Trails To

Hoosier Heritage

Other Books By The Author

The Lost Dutchman Mine: A Short Story Of A Tall Tale

Survival In The Wilds

Works In Progress

The Lost Adams Gold Diggings

Along The Dutchman Treasure Trail

The Dutchman's Lost Mine

Treasure Of El Sombrero

Trails To Hoosier Heritage

by

Harry G. Black

Published by HMB Publications
7406 Monroe Avenue
Hammond, Indiana 46324

Library of Congress Catalog Card Number 80-81608
ISBN: 0-937086-00-2

Printed by
RUSS' PRINT SHOP
131 N. Main St. ★ Hebron, Indiana 46341

The want of a vacationland should not be foiled
by a limited pocketbook. Your own vicinity,
county, and state holds wonders to be seen and
pleasures to be enjoyed. Oftentimes these nearby
attractions exceeds one's highest expectations.

JDL

Table Of Contents

Foreword

Trails To Hoosier Heritage is a book that makes historic Indiana come alive for the readers. Author Harry Black of Hammond, Indiana successfully focuses the public's attention on the early Indiana settlers that have remained buried in the pages of county history books. This I think is admirable, because we too often read about the historic leaders of our state and pay little heed to the hard working pioneers that made Indiana their home.

Harry brings this message across to his readers when he writes: "The unsung heros of Indiana's past and its present day are the people. The people that live in the towns, cities, and in the countryside. Most of us are familar with the paintings of the old country churches on the hilltops. They can still be seen if you take the time to travel the byways of this nation. Usually you will find a cemetery alongside, behind, or across the road from the churches. Whenever I walk through these silent resting places glancing at the dates on the stones, I wonder what these individuals from the 1800's could tell us. The story we do know is that today's life style was made possible through their efforts. They are the ones that filled the ranks of the armies, they are the ones that cleared the land and plowed the fields, they are the ones that put their shoulders to the grindstone in the primitive factories of that day. They are the ones that should be immortalized."

Black interlaces some of the popular historical attractions with a number of lesser known historic sites. I must admit, that even I, am not acquainted with all his listings. In each of his entries Black gives the readers what has happened in the past, what there is of that past today, and how to get there.

The author writes about his own travels hunting a lost Indian treasure cave and finding an old metal smelter. He successfully proves that adventuring in Indiana is an exciting and thrilling experience.

Black puts forth in the introduction of his book why people should travel in Indiana. He states: "It gives jobs to fellow Hoosiers, increases your knowledge of your own state, saves energy, and last but not least, saves you money."

Harry, without any equivocation, writes that Indiana is a vacationer's mecca. An Indiana vacation, I believe, will give credence to this statement.

Ron Gegenheimer
Manager, North 40
Park Camp Grounds
Chesterfield, Indiana

December 16, 1980

Preface

Harry Black, has in this book given the readers an overview of Indiana's history. He takes you back to the time when the French explorers first penetrated the northern reaches of the state, he carries you through Indiana's involvement in the French and Indian War, tells you about the American campaigns that took place in the state during the Revolutionary War, and gives glimpses of frontier towns springing up, fighting for survival, and either declining or going on to become a commercial success.

The author has personally visited all the sites that he has written about in his book. Black readily admits that it would take volumes to span Indiana's history, but in his own unique way he gives you an enjoyable, interesting, and knowledgeable picture of the state's background. He has tried, and I would say with success, to give his readers many of the points of historical interest across the state. Every entry in the book has a summary of its past, an overview of the historic attractions to be seen at the location, and how to reach it.

Black should be applauded for the way he presents his material because he leaves it to you, the reader, to make detailed plans of your Indiana explorations. In my mind planning is half the fun of the trip. All the members of the family or group can participate in this endeavor. This type of project certainly lends itself to the feeling of togetherness.

I would say Black's new work merits the title of **Trails To Hoosier Heritage.** His insights into the subject matter reveal his curiosity as a researcher, his eye for details, and his ability to present in a stimulating manner the sites written about and photographed. Historical and modern day Indiana blend themselves into a vacationer's paradise. Black's new work is an avenue to this utopia.

Milton F. Rose
Researcher of American
and Mexican History
Phoenix, Arizona

December 5, 1980

Acknowledgements

The following people and organizations are graciously thanked for their help and cooperation in the preparation of this manuscript. They are: Carol Clark, Jeanette Carr, Kathleen Diehl, and Marjorie Sohl of the Hammond, Indiana Public Library; Mrs. Leona T. Alig, Manuscript Librarian, and staff of the Indiana Historical Society Library in Indianapolis, Indiana; the Indiana State Library, Indianapolis, Indiana; the Lake County Public Library, Merrillville, Indiana; Dr. John B. Patton, Indiana State Geologist; Mary Beth Fox, secretary of Dr. Patton; Hazel M. White of Kansas City, Missouri; Robert G. Bradshaw of Delphi, Indiana; Jean Headik of Kirklin, Indiana; Jim and Dixie McDonough of Madison, Indiana; Margaret H. Dow of Madison, Indiana; Howard I. Eldon of the Madison County Historical Society; Mrs. Birney G. Bailey of the Brown County Historical Society; Bonnie Murphy of the Randolph County Historical Society; L. Rex Myers of Washington, Indiana; Carol Waddell of the Tippecanoe County Historical Association; Ruby Stiles of the Martin County Historical Society; R. B. Whitsitt of the Cass County Historical Society; Henry L. Link of Waterloo, Indiana; Dow Baker of Waterloo, Indiana; Cecil J. Smith of Salem, Indiana; Lester and Jane Tweedle of Brownsburg, Indiana; Dorothy J. Clark of the Vigo County Historical Society; Susan Davison of Columbia City, Indiana; Mrs. E. E. Hass of Springfield, Illinois; John J. Fierst of the Dubois County Historical Society; Mrs. Roy M. Pritchard of Belleville, Indiana; Miss Paulette Hayes of Historic Connorsville, Inc.; Bill DeCoursey of Minneapolis, Minnesota; Ronald L. Woodward of the Wabash County Historical Society; Shirley Willard of the Fulton County Historical Society; Mildred B. Blake of Wadesville, Indiana; Mrs. J. W. Snowden of Rockville, Indiana; Kathryn O. Malone of the Park County Museum; Thurlo C. Holcomb of the Noble County Historical Society; the Historic Hoosier Hills of Versailles, Indiana; Garry Schalliol of the Bartholomew County Historical Society; Kenneth D. Sever of Waldon, Indiana; John R. Funk of the George Ade Memorial Association; Dorothy Arbuckle of the Newton County Historical Society; James Broadhurst of Valparaiso, Indiana; Mrs. Chauncey Brockway Baldwin of the Elkhart County Historical Society; Milton F. Rose of Phoenix, Arizona; Julius Buettner of Jasper, Indiana; David E. Horn, Archivist, Ray O. West Library, DePauw University; Paul W. Thomas, Director of Archives, Archives and Historical Library, Marion, Indiana; James C. Sullivan, Director of the Northern Indiana Historical Library, South Bend, Indiana; the Elkhart County Park and Recreation Department; the Lake County Park and Recreation Department; the Indiana Dunes National Lakeshore; and the Indiana Department of Natural Resources, Division of Museums and Memorials, and Division of State Parks.

Several Indiana newspapers gave me assistance in the completion of this book. They are: the **Post Tribune,** Gary, Indiana; **The Times,** Hammond, Indiana; the **Indianapolis News** and **Star,** Indianapolis,

Indiana; the **Salem Democrat,** Salem, Indiana; the **Shelbyville News,** Shelbyville, Indiana; the **South Bend Tribune,** South Bend, Indiana; the **Terre Haute Tribune,** Terre Haute, Indiana; and the **Tri-State Trader,** Knightstown, Indiana.

The photography work for the book was done by Warren Black, Ron Gegenheimer, John Grzeczka, Chuck Pearson, Larry Swentzel, and the author.

Warren Black drew the sketch for the cover of the book.

I would be amiss without naming my traveling companions that helped make my Indiana sojourns so delightful. They are: Jay Abate, Myron Black, Warren Black, Roland Camp, Kenneth and Martha Emrick, Hank (Floyd) Ford, Charles Freeman, Jim Galus, Ron Gegenheimer, John Grzeczka, Jim Kovecsi, Leona Nowak, Michael O'Connell, Chuck Pearson, Joe Smelko, Brian Smith, Fred and Mary Smith, Larry and Gaye Jean Swentzel, Joe and Muriel Wauro, my wife Marilyn, grandson Jamie, and my white Spitz Dog Waggie.

Introduction

In the late 1960's and early 1970's Indiana high school Social Studies teachers were using a movie in their classrooms titled, "Indiana Has Everything." The film gave an overview of the state featuring the coal mines and stone quarries in the south, the central Indiana farm belt, and the heavy industrialization in the northern tier of Hoosierland. Indiana was correctly portrayed as an urbanized, industrialized, and agricultural state.

When the 1976 Bicentennial was upon us many Hoosiers started becoming cognizant of the tremendous events that happened within the confines of their state. Some of us even found out our state was named Indiana because its area was known as the "Land of the Indians."

My interest in Indiana's history was stimulated by an evening's conversation that I had in a prospector's cabin on the west end of the Superstition Mountains in Arizona. The idea of writing a book about the Hoosier State was implanted on my mind that fateful night.

Broadly speaking, Indiana does have a great diversity in industry and agriculture. With a few exceptions, the state has been economically and physically richly blessed.

Indiana's frontier history is equal to any that can be found in the nation. The state's march in time from its frontier to where we are today is a fascinating parade of characters and events. **Trails To Hoosier Heritage** gives glimpses of this intriguing history.

I have traveled the length and breadth of Indiana in writing this book. Every location mentioned herein has been personally visited by me. Many sites that I write about are lesser known and on the byways of the state. I must admit I have a penchant for the out-of-the-way places.

Hoosier travelers interested in the more popular points of historical interest in the state are accomodated by numerous entries in the book of such locations. I have been impressed by the staff personnel at these better known attractions. They make a sincere effort to make your visit one that is informative and enjoyable.

Indiana is a vacationer's mecca. Tourism is a growing industry in the state. Travel in Indiana: It gives jobs to fellow Hoosiers; increases your knowledge of your state; saves energy; and last but not least, saves you money.

It is my hope that this book opens up new Indiana vistas for your idle time enjoyment.

Harry G. Black

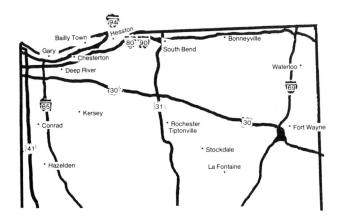

Newton County's Lost Community Conrad

YOU CAN SPOT the town of Conrad on recent road maps of Indiana, between Enos and Lake Village, off U. S. 41 in Newton County. Go there and you will have difficulty in finding even sparse remnants of a town, however.

Hardly enough remains to qualify it as a ghost town, but if a ghost stalked there it would likely be the wraith of Jennie Conrad, the town's founder whose strange character also brought its doom.

In 1852, wealthy land investor and cattleman Lemuel Milk of Kankakee, IL., and partners bought 40,000 acres in northern Newton County, Indiana. Much of it was covered by shallow Beaver Lake, which they drained.

Lemuel and Mary Milk had six children. Jennie was the first. Her parents sent her to exclusive schools, and she became an elegant woman in some respects, but was eccentric and fiercely headstrong.

Jennie was 29 in September of 1878 when she was married to George Conrad, 40, a Chicago bank cashier. The wedding was the most elaborate ever held in Kankakee. After a gala reception, the wedding party traveled in a private railroad car to Chicago.

In the early 1880's the bride's father gave George and Jennie 4,000 acres of his land in Newton County. The Conrads followed in Lemuel Milk's footsteps, taking up the cattle and land business.

They made their home two miles south of Lake Village and called it

Dune Oak. Jennie furnished her home with nothing but the best, including imported china and silver.

Both George and Jennie proved adept at business, raising cattle for the Chicago market and renting unused land to other livestock owners for grazing. Jennie has been called the originator of the Spotted Poland China breed of hogs. She also has been credited with inventing the six or eight bottom plow, which was pulled by a steam tractor.

The Conrads had a son whom they named Platt, using Jennie's mother's maiden name.

Soon after the Conrads arrived in Newton County, Jennie took an

Stair steps that once led up to the entrance of the two room, red brick, Conrad school.

extreme dislike to the nearby hamlet of Lake Village. Whether she saw this struggling village as a threat to plans of her own to start a town or had personal conflicts with some of the citizens of Lake Village is not known. She often went to the more distant towns of Schneider and Lowell to board the train for Chicago rather than catch it at the Lake Village station. She had her mail addressed to Morocco, sending a horseman on a 36-mile round trip to Morocco several times a week because she didn't like it brought by a Lake Village rural route carrier.

After George Conrad died in 1896, Jennie expanded her business activities. She mortgaged her original holdings of 4,000 acres to buy 3,000 more.

The town of Conrad was platted in 1904. Jennie used her own

resources to build it. A 2.7-acre plot laid out in the center of town was called Platt Park in honor of her son. She named streets for herself, her mother, her husband and other relatives.

Jennie undoubtedly dreamed of Conrad becoming a thriving community, but it never was more than a small village.

At its zenith, Conrad consisted of an 18-room hotel, blacksmith shop, combination store and post office, concrete block factory, church, school, stockyards and several residences.

The stock pens at Conrad shipped thousands of head of cattle to Chicago. Jennie fought for a railroad depot for Conrad. The Chicago, Indiana, and Southern Railroad finally consented to have passenger trains stop there, after Jennie had agreed to build the depot, which she did.

In 1906, the railroad was bought by the New York Central.

Taking great pride in her new empire; Jennie had all her town structures painted yellow. These included the public buildings, her own ranch house and tenant farm buildings. The wheels and spokes on her wagons and carriages also were her favorite color, a shade of yellow some town folks remembered as "mustard" and others, "bright orange."

The fate of Conrad was sealed through Jennie's own irascible temperament. She constantly had difficulties with her hired help, demanding more than they were prepared to give and never satisfied by their work. At times her tenant farmers would quit in the middle of the growing season. Jennie's hiring and firing of people, combined with resignations, made for a continual turnover of her employees.

When Jennie was not fighting with her help, she was feuding with her neighbors. She frequently was in court over spats with townspeople.

Jennie once was heavily fined for confiscating a farmer's cattle and nearly causing their death by refusing to feed and water them. The farmer, after picking corn for Jennie, had turned his cattle into the barren field, incurring Jennie's wrath.

Jennie became a Newton County legend, often seen dressed in black, with a shotgun by her side, whisking about her property in a carriage pulled by two spirited horses. According to the legend, she began taking the shotgun with her after an incident or two when employees did not take her orders seriously. Thereafter, she was accepted as boss.

Once she caught some boys stealing blackberries from her fields. The lads had filled several small containers with berries. Jennie pulled her horses to a halt, jumped from the carriage and grabbed the berry containers from the boys. She poured the berries out on the dirt, crushed them with her feet, and ordered the boys off her property.

In retaliation, the boys burned a 40-acre tract of ripe wheat.

In the late 1930's the railroad pulled out a track maintenance crew that was quartered in Conrad. This reduced the population to a mere handful of citizens. One by one they refused to live in Conrad or work for Jennie because of her arrogance.

Conrad was almost deserted by the time Jennie died in 1939, at the home of a niece in Rensselaer. The railroad depot was the only building still in use. It remained in operation until the early 1940's.

Jennie's son, Platt, became a well known stockbroker in Chicago. He rarely visited his childhood home in Newton County because he, too, ended up bitterly fighting with his mother.

Soon after Jennie's death, Platt married the woman, Lena by name, who had been his secretary for many years. Platt and Lena Conrad apparently had no plans of becoming landed gentry in Newton County. They continued to live in Chicago, and when Platt died in the early 1950s, the remaining 3,000 acres of land in Newton County went to his widow. Mother Jennie, apparently pressed for cash in her declining years, had sold 4,000 acres of the estate. Lena Conrad died about ten years ago, and since the couple had no children, the property is held by a Chicago trust company, its exact status unknown.

Reminiscing about Conrad while visiting the town-site recently was Edwin R. Robinson of Morocco, a retired Newton County attorney who had lived in Conrad as a child.

His parents, Rufus and Ina Robinson, were New York Central station agents there and owned their own home in Conrad.

Edwin Robinson said the town probably never had more than 30 residents at any one time. Many residents were section hands living in the New York Central boarding house just north of the depot.

Robinson pointed out the railroad depot's ruins. The outline of the freight room and passenger station still are discernible.

Conrad's first school was a one room wooden building. Later a two room brick school replaced it. The only remnant left of the latter school is the concrete front steps. Bricks from this building were used in constructing an addition to the Lake Village school.

Robinson, who once was the lone Conrad school's first-grader, was graduated from the eighth grade there, and remembers teachers Edna Menter, Zella Bess Magee and Lee H. Crane. Mr. Robinson stated, "Ewing Best drove a horse drawn school bus that brought kids from miles around."

"I remember when we were kids," he continued, "we would take sticks and twist up the bottoms of our trousers with them. This would bag our pants with a tight fit around the ankles. We would stuff the blackberries we picked into our trousers. Jennie could never tell we had the berries, but she would yank the sticks out and let the berries fall out on the ground."

Mrs. Jennie Conrad's body rests in a mausoleum she built in Mound Grove Cemetery in Kankakee. Although only a few foundation ruins remain of her town, her name probably will forever be associated with Newton County because of the drainage channel that runs on the west side of U. S. 41 near the townsite, named Conrad Ditch.

To reach the site of Conrad take U. S. Route 41 south out of Hammond, Indiana across the Kankakee River into Newton County. Continue south on route 41 past its junction with Indiana Route 10. A few miles south of this intersection you will see a yellow farm house on the right, or west side, of route 41. Just past the house watch for a highway sign indicating a side road coming from the west and junctioning with route 41. A short distance past the road sign will be a crossover road heading east. Turn left or east on this road and crossover route 41's north bound lanes. Follow the dirt road east over the north-south running railroad tracks. Here it will junction with another dirt road running north alongside the track bed. Turn north on this road paralleling the railroad tracks. Drive slowly and watch for the railroad depot and hotel foundation ruins on your right hand (east) side. They are just a short distance up the roadway. Conrad's other ruins can be found by searching the areas to the east and west of the railroad tracks in this vicinity.

George Ade

Flowing through Indiana's history is a remarkable parade of authors. Among the onetime best-selling Hoosiers are Edward Eggleston, Charles Major, Ross Lockridge, Jr., Gen. Lew Wallace, Gene Stratton Porter, James Whitcomb Riley, Booth Tarkington, Theodore Dreiser, Ernie Pyle and George Ade.

At the height of their popularity they all moved American readers to cheers, jeers and tears.

Why such a proliferation of writers from the Hoosier state? One writer claimed "it was something in the water." The "pollen from the horse weed along the Wabash River," said another; and the "good soil of the state," a third claimed. The career of George Ade, author and playwright from Newton County, IN., is a study in the whims of literary fate. Ade is specifically remembered for his book "Fables in Slang" and smash-hit plays such as "The College Widow" and "The Sultan of Sulu."

Ade was born Feb. 9, 1866 in Kentland, IN., son of John and Adaline Ade, the second youngest in a family of three boys and three girls.

Before George was born the family had lived in Morocco, IN., where his father was employed as postmaster and blacksmith.

When Newton County was formed out of part of Jasper County the Ade family moved to Kentland. John Ade was elected Newton County recorder and later became an employee of the Kentland bank.

John Ade's employment provided little money for luxuries. At times Adaline Ade had to wash the children's under-clothing at night and dry them by the stove because there was only enough money for one suit of clothes per child.

George Ade developed an early appreciation of the stage when he attended performances of repertoire companies, based in Indianapolis, which played in small towns. Ade sometimes gained admission to McCullough's Hall in Kentland to watch the plays by passing out handbills announcing the engagement.

In October, 1881, George wrote a high school theme titled "A Basket of Potatoes." The theme compared life to a basket of potatoes. He wrote that when the basket was jolted the big potatoes rose to the top and the small ones went to the bottom. In order to get to the top in life, or be a "big potato," one must be "educated, honest, observing, and careful," he said.

George's teacher was so impressed by the composition she asked John Ade's permission to have it published in the local newspaper. This was George Ade's first published work.

John Ade was perplexed when the county superintendent of schools suggested to him that George should go to college upon graduation from high school. Friends said it would be a waste of money.

Many who knew George thought he was somewhat of a dreamer and couldn't even be trusted with the cows. John Ade thought that the newly-organized Purdue University in Lafayette, with its emphasis on agriculture and mechanic arts, might be a good place for George. At least he would be exposed to several occupations.

Ade applied for a county scholarship for his son in the fall of 1882. George was granted the stipend and started his freshman year at Purdue University in September 1883.

While attending Purdue, George struck up a friendship with John T. McCutcheon. The two university students had no idea that their meeting would evolve into a long relationship.

John McCutcheon became one of the nation's leading cartoonists and journalists with the Chicago Tribune. He probably is best remembered for his "Injun Summer" cartoon.

George graduated from Purdue University on June 9, 1887, and immediately went to work in a Lafayette attorney's office preparing for a career in law. After seven weeks he gave up the idea of becoming a lawyer.

Ade began his journalism career with the Lafayette Morning News. The paper folded and George got a job on the staff of an evening newspaper named The Call. He later took a job with a patent medicine firm, where he wrote advertisements and answered correspondence.

John McCutcheon went to Chicago in the fall of 1889 and obtained a job in the art department of the Chicago Morning News. He wrote enticing letters to Ade urging him to join him in the "big city."

Ade lost his job with the patent medicine company when it changed management, and marched off to join McCutcheon in Chicago in June of 1890.

John McCutcheon got an interview for Ade with the city editor of the Morning News and George was hired as a cub reporter. His first assignment was writing the daily weather report.

Ade had found a home. He covered the gamut of reporting fires, police activities, and sporting events. Ade and McCutcheon then got the idea of saving part of their salary each week for a trip to Europe. The city editor of the Morning News agreed to let them go with continued salaries, providing they would send him two illustrated articles each week. On this condition, both men eventually made several world journeys.

One of Ade's later duties was writing a column called "Stories of the Streets and of the Town." The column concerned the daily life of Chicago in the 1890s.

In 1892 the Morning News became the News-Record. Shortly thereafter the name was shortened to the Record.

Ade's first fable appeared in the Record on Sept. 17, 1897. It was apparent to the reading public that he was clowning around. The fable generated no popular demand for more of the same. Ade later rewrote it and called it "The Fable of Sister Mae Who Did Well As Could Be Expected."

The Chicago Publishing firm of Herbert S. Stone and Co. previously had published three books titled, "Artie," "Pink Marsh," and "Doc Thorne" from material taken from Ade's daily column, and had exacted a promise from Ade to write a full-length book. Ade and publisher had agreed on the subject matter and title. A novel, possibly the "great American novel," would be called "The College Widow." Dummy book covers with "The College Widow" imprinted upon them, and carrying only blank pages in between, were made up. Stone Company's salesmen carried "Fools Gold" copies (dummies) to book dealers, soliciting orders. Advance orders started coming in for the yet-to-be-written novel.

But George wasn't yet ready to give up his weekly pay check from the paper for the promise of future royalties. The great American novel was going to have to wait.

The publisher, knowing Ade couldn't deliver on the novel, urged George to write enough fables to make a book. They would call the publication "Fables in Slang."

Ade saw this as a way out of his dilemma with his publisher and more and more fables started appearing in his column "Stories of the Street and of the Town." They ran about once a week between July and October of 1899.

The Record took advantage of the situation and started selling some of the fables to other newspapers. George Ade was given a raise to $65 a week, top salary for a reporter.

"Fables in Slang" was published by Herbert S. Stone & Co. in the fall of 1899. Within a year approximately 70,000 copies were sold. George Ade was on his way to becoming independently wealthy and famous.

The publisher brought out another Ade book, titled "More Fables," in the fall of 1900. Altogether, Ade wrote 10 volumes of fables between 1899 and 1920.

Ade was capable of satirizing events unique to the individual but common in everyday life, such as courting, marrying, and employment. In some cases, the fable expressed in satire the hopelessness of breaking the

George Ade's Hazelden Manor.

bondage imposed on the individual by his own social class, or the composite social structure.

At the end of each fable there was a moral. However, readers in some instances had a hard time relating the moral to the text of the fables.

Ade, now able to break away from the paper, sought refuge to work in Newton County. He selected and bought a plot of land two miles east of Brook, bordering the Iroquois River.

Ade wanted to construct a modest bungalow for his retreat. But somehow his plans went awry and a two-story, many-roomed, English Tudor style mansion was built. Construction did not stop with the house. Soon to follow were a combination garage and stable, a swimming pool and shower house, a green house, a cow barn, a caretaker's cottage, a store room, and a huge water tank.

Ade furnished the house to suit his own tastes. He proudly displayed souveniers he had collected on his world travels. Among these were colorful tapestries, Chinese porcelain, and unusual ivory carvings, all located on the first floor of the home. The second floor was furnished in early American.

In 1904, when most people were still using an "outhouse," Ade installed modern plumbing, including a shower and marble shower stall in his home. One of the first telephones in Newton County was placed in the Ade home.

Ade called his retreat "Hazelden Farm." Hazelden was a modification of the name Hazleton, taken from his family background.

Hazelden Farm fell into disrepair after Ade's death in 1944. Vandals attacked it and left the place in shambles. The Newton County Historical Society has successfully restored the mansion to its original spendor, and now conducts tours of the home.

Ade, an early golf addict, had a nine hole golf course laid out for his weekend guests. The Hazelden Country Club was started by him for the purpose of giving residents of the area access to a golf course.

Fame did not change Ade too much. Often during the week he would drop in at the barber shop in Brook for a shave. He invited neighbors to call on him when they were out his way. It was said that if a person knocked on the door of the mansion instead of walking directly in he was a stranger.

It was not unusual for George Ade to arrange employment for his friends or give them money. He sometimes sent money by mail to persons who made requests for help by mail, even though he hardly knew them.

George Ade remained a bachelor all his life. An early love affair that failed to materialize into marriage seemed to have a lasting effect on him.

McCutcheon and Ade were instrumental in forming the organization called the "Indiana Society of Chicago." Membership was composed of Hoosiers who had migrated to Chicago and some of the organization's social outings were held at Hazelden Farm. The society still is active.

Ade had not forgotten "The College Widow," but wrote it as a play instead of a novel. "The College Widow" was a smashing box office success. Ade went on to write 11 other plays. Among them were "The Sultan of Sulu," "Peggy from Paris," "Sho-Gun," and "The County Chairman." Of the 12 plays he wrote, nine of them were considered successful.

Early in the 1920s Ade wrote several full-length motion pictures. Three of these, "Leading Citizen," "Back Home and Broke," and "Woman Proof" brought him a fortune in royalties.

Davis Ross, former Purdue graduate and inventor of an improved steering gear for automobiles, teamed up with Ade in 1928 to buy the land for a new Purdue football stadium. They contributed additional sums for the construction of the sports arena. It was named "Ross-Ade Stadium" in their honor.

George Ade died on May 14, 1944 in Brook, at the age of 78. His papers were willed to Purdue University, and trustees of the estate gave Ades house along with 10 landscaped acres to Newton County for a George Ade Memorial Hospital.

Ade must have thought his literary work would not survive, otherwise he would not have said this about the Ross-Ade Stadium as quoted by Fred Kelly in "George Ade, Warmhearted Satirist:"

"Students who come here a few years from now will know nothing about a fellow named Ade who wrote fables in slang, and plays, but if my name is . . . on that stadium, they'll be tipped off that someone named Ade was identified in some way with Purdue University."

George Ade's home was placed on the National Register of Historical Places in 1976. Tours of Ade's mansion can be arranged by writing to the George Ade Memorial Association, Incorporated, Post Office Box 103, Kentland, Indiana 47951.

The Ade manor is located on Indiana Route 16, two miles to the east of Brook, Indiana. It is on the south side of the highway just to the east of the George Ade Memorial Hospital.

Town of Bailly
Porter County

The first permanent settler in what is now the Calumet Region of Indiana was a French fur trader by the name of Joseph Bailly. He established his home and fur trading post on the north bank of the Little Calumet River in Porter County in 1822. Accompaning him was his wife, Marie, and their five children.

Joseph Bailly and his family were according to most records, the only settlers in the Calumet Region between 1822 and 1832. His trading post located on a principle Indian trail, became a meeting place for the Indians and trappers. Bailly opened an inn which serviced travelers passing over the old post road between Detroit and Chicago. In 1833 there were approximately eight log cabins along the Little Calumet River near Bailly's trading post.

Mrs. Bailly, because of her Ottawa Indian lineage, was a great asset to Bailly's trading activities with the Indians. The Potawatomie and Ottawa Indians were known to camp for months in the vicinity of the Bailly homestead.

Bailly, knowing that his fur trading business was finished when the

*A view of the concrete block walls that form the
square of the Bailly Cemetery.*

Indians were removed to the west, platted a town along the north bank of the Little Calumet River. He proudly called it, "Town of Bailly." The new settlers, preferring the better agricultural land to the south, turned their backs on Bailly's dream town. Undaunted in his hopes for his new settlement, Bailly passed away in 1835.

The Bailly homestead remained in the family until 1918. It passed through a number of owners until it was acquired by the Indiana Dunes National Lakeshore in 1971.

A prerequisite for a visit to the Bailly Homestead is a stop at the National Lakeshore's Visitor Center located at Kemil Road and U. S. Route 12 in Porter County. Here you can obtain personal instructions and written information on how to reach the home site. The visitor center is open from 8 to 4:30 during the fall, winter, and spring seasons. In the summer months these hours are extended.

Today, the Bailly Homestead is composed of five buildings, the main house, three replicas of the log structures that once stood on the site, and a second brick home built by the family at a later date. The original Bailly home was a two and one half story hewn oak building. Over the years descendents of Joseph Bailly added rooms and modernized the structure. The log cabin which is adjacent to the main house is a replica of the old kitchen which was later converted into a chapel in honor of Joseph and Marie Bailly. North of the chapel is a replica of the log building that was the coachman's house. Across from the main house is a small log storehouse which is similar to the one that Bailly had constructed to house the goods of the Indians while they were on their hunting expeditions.

A short hike through the rolling woodlands north of the homestead will bring you to the most unusual Bailly Cemetery. Here on the top of a small hill the Bailly family constructed a square concrete block wall. The ground inside the square was either leveled off or filled in to bring it to the approximate hieght of the walls. Burials were made in the square and along the outer facing of the parallelogram.

The Indiana Dunes National Lakeshore offers numerous activities for your enjoyment. Some of these are swimming, hiking, bicycle riding, horseback riding, and picnicking. For more information write to the Indiana Dunes National Lakeshore, 1100 North Mineral Springs Road, Porter, Indiana 46304.

To reach the Indiana Dunes National Lakeshore take Interstate Route 94 east out of Gary until it junctions with Indiana Route 49. Turn north on route 49 to U. S. Route 12. At this intersection turn east and drive three miles to route 12's junction with Kemil Road. The visitor center is on the southwest corner of this intersection.

The South Shore Railroad provides commuter service to the Indiana Dunes National Lakeshore from Chicago, Illinois, South Bend, Indiana, and points in between. Mini-buses are provided on the week ends by the national lakeshore during the summer months to shuttle visitors to the many points of interest. For more information about the train service to the national lakeshore contact the ticket agent at the nearest South Shore Railroad Station.

Bonneyville
Elkhart County

Edward William Bonney and his young wife arrived in Elkhart County in the early 1830's. Bonney entertained ideas of founding his own community which he planned to name after himself. His first move in this direction was to purchase an 80 acre tract of land along the Little Elkhart River. Knowing that his settlement would need some type of industry to draw people Bonney constructed a saw and grist mill. Bonney named his settlement Bonneyville.

Approximately 10 homes were built in the vicinity of the grist mill. Bonney anticipated rapid growth of his community when the railroad reached the settlement. As in so many other cases, the railroad saw fit to bypass the village. Bonneyville, as a town, was on a collision course with obscurity.

Bonneyville Mill.

In 1842 Edward William Bonney was arrested for counterfeiting money. He managed to escape justice by breaking out of jail. The next few years of his life were spent as an outcast along the Mississippi River Valley.

Bonney had a chance to redeem himself during the American Civil War. The Federal Government pardoned Bonney for his crime when he joined the Union Army. Bonney died in 1864 and was buried in the Bonneyville Cemetery.

The Bonneyville grist mill has been in continuous operation since 1832. In 1968 the Elkhart County Chapter of the Michiana Watershed saved the old mill from destruction when it purchased the site through public subscription. The organization turned the site over to the Elkhart County Park and Recreation Board in November of 1969. On October 22, 1976 the Bonneyville Mill was placed on the National Register of Historic Places by the United States Department of Interior in cooperation with the Indiana Department of Natural Resources, Division of Historical Preservation.

Today, the 155 acre Bonneyville Mill County Park offers you an excursion into the past along with the enjoyments of the present. The mill, which is open daily May through October, still uses water power to grind corn, wheat, buckwheat, and rye. Visitors can purchase flours and meal at the mill.

The park has facilities for picnicking, hiking, fishing, and playground activities. Shelters are available on a first come basis or by reservation. For more information write to the Elkhart County Park and Recreation Department, 113 North Third Street, Goshen, Indiana 46526.

To reach Bonneyville Mill County Park take Indiana Route 120 east out of Bristol, Indiana until it intersects with County Road 131. Turn south on 131 to the park.

Chesterton
Porter County

In January of 1835 the first post office in the Calumet Region of Indiana was established at a village named Coffee Creek. This hamlet eventually became present day Chesterton. The post office was named after a small creek by that name that ran through the area.

Between the years of 1837 and 1846 the post office was opened and closed two times. In 1849 the name of the Coffee Creek post office was changed to Calumet. The village that was

Thomas Centennial Park's band shell.

laid out in 1852 took the name Calumet in deference to the post office.

In the late 1860's Calumet changed its name to Chesterton. The residents found that many people associated Calumet with the two rivers by that name that ran in the general vicinity of the village. Not to be outdone the post office switched its name to Chesterton in 1870.

Chesterton, because of its excellent railroad connections, became the home of several industries in the latter half of the nineteenth century. The Hillstrom Organ Company became the town's main industry when it moved its plant from Chicago to Chesterton in the early 1880's. With the discovery or rich clay deposits, three brickyards were opened in the area. A paint factory opened its doors in Chesterton in the early 1890's. Some people believed that Chesterton would become the industrial giant of the Calumet Region.

Sadly, the economic ups and downs over the years took their toll on Chesterton's industries. Businesses closed, others changed hands, and the dream of Chesterton becoming the industrial hub of Northwest Indiana passed quietly into history by the early 1920's.

Chesterton today, while being in the Calumet area, offers that small town atmosphere that many residents of the large cities seek out. The town is clean, well kept, and has a bustling downtown shopping district. An old band shell stands in the middle of the Thomas Centennial Park located along the railroad tracks in the center of the town. Benches line the pathways through the park. Occasionally you can see the oldsters of the community sitting on them soaking up the sunshine. One wonders what tales they have to tell.

Located a short distance to the west of the park is the old railroad freight station. A discriminating eye will be able to see that the spacious station was once a busy shipping and transferring point. It now houses shops that sell paintings, painting supplies, new and used books, antiques, plants, and sculptures. There is an old-time ice cream parlor and sandwich shop in town that will bring back memories to the older generations and will be an experience out of the past for youngsters. Numerous antique, gift, and craft shops await your Chesterton visit.

To reach Chesterton take Indiana Route 49 south off of Interstate Route 94 or north off of Interstate Routes 80 and 90. When route 49 junctions with Indian Boundry Road turn west on Indian Boundry until it intersects with Calumet Avenue. Turn south on Calumet Avenue to the downtown shopping district.

Deep River
Lake County

In 1835, John Wood, a native of Massachusetts, left the east with his cousin John Barker to seek their fortunes in the Northwest. The pair traveled by boat on the Great Lakes and landed at the trading post where Michigan City, Indiana now stands. Barker elected to remain at the trading post while Wood explored the surrounding area for a mill site. In December of 1835 Wood found a location for his mill on a wide and deep stream which flowed on the eastern edge of present day Lake County. It is now known as Deep River.

Wood then returned east to bring his wife, Hannah, and their children to their new home. In 1837 he built a sawmill. The following year Wood constructed the first grist mill in the area. This was the beginning of industry in Lake and Porter Counties. Farmers from miles around brought their grain to be ground at the grist mill.

John Wood's Grist Mill.

Wood's Mill was the first name given to this site. It was changed to Woodvale, and finally to Deep River when a post office was established there in 1838. On September 10, 1895 the above two words were combined and the town's name was spelled Deepriver. Today, the village is again known as Deep River. The post office has been but a memory for years.

John Wood was active in his community. In February of 1843 he was appointed to be one of the viewers to locate the state road running from Porter County, through Deep River, and then on to Chicago. The Old Lincoln Highway is presumed to be part of this road.

Deep River prospered. Wood set aside a two acre public common to the west of his mill. A shoe shop, blacksmith shop, and a general store were built around the common. Wood refused to lay out town lots for sale to the public because he was afraid a tavern might be built on one of them. In later years a cheese factory and one of the first automobile garages in the area opened in the town.

The mill and the country store were the center of the social and economic life of the community. People gathered at both places to exchange news and gossip.

John Wood's son, Milton, succeeded his father as miller. He operated the mill until his retirement.

My wife Marilyn, nephew Fred Smith, and I discovered the old Wood's mill on one of our back road drives in the late 1960's. We explored and photographed the brick mill building. At that time we talked about the possibility of someone restoring it. We had no idea this would actually happen.

The Lake County Parks and Recreation Department, seeing the need for preserving our history, restored John Wood's mill for the United States Bicentennial. Today, the old grist mill is once again grinding corn into cornmeal. Those interested can purchase a bag of this freshly ground cornmeal on the main floor of the old mill. The second and third stories of the mill now house a nineteenth century museum. An art gallery is located on the fourth floor of the building. An old church building to the west of the mill has been remodeled into an interpretive center for the Deep River County Park. The park has a canoe livery service, hiking trails, horseback trails, and picnic areas. For further information write to the Lake County Parks and Recreation Department, 2293 North Main Street, Crown Point, Indiana 46307.

John Wood's grist mill was placed on the National Register of Historical Places on October 10, 1975.

To reach the Deep River County Park take U. S. Route 30 east out of Merrillville, Indiana. Continue east on route 30 past its junction with Interstate Route 65 until you reach its junction with Randolph Street. Turn north on Randolph until it intersects with County Road 330. Follow Route 330 east to the mill.

Historic Fort Wayne
Allen County

The capital or principle village of the Miami Indian tribe, named Ke-ki-o-que, in the Miami language, was located where the present city of Fort Wayne now stands. Here the St. Mary's and St. Joseph Rivers unite to form the Maumee River. LaSalle was said to have portaged here in 1669 or 1670. French fur traders following LaSalle's footsteps built an outpost at this site in 1690.

Ke-ki-o-que became known as the "French Stores," as it was for a long time a place of resort for many traders. Voyageurs would stop there as they portaged from the Maumee River to the Wabash River.

The British took the outpost from the French in 1760 during the French and Indian War (1754-1763). Three years later Chief Pontiac's warriors seized the fort from the British. The fort returned to British hands at the close of Pontiac's Uprising in 1765.

Historic Fort Wayne.

During the American Revolution (1775-1783) the three rivers site, then known as Miamitown, saw the coming and going of opposing armies. In October of 1778, Colonel Henry Hamilton and his British forces stopped there on their way to attack the American held fort in Vincennes. Hamilton was successful in capturing the Vincennes military installation, but lost it to George Rogers Clark in February of 1779.

In 1780, a French soldier of fortune named LaBalme led a small army of Creoles from Vincennes to attack the British at Detroit. LaBalme's forces stopped on their trek long enough to capture and destroy Miamitown. The great Miami Chief Little Turtle led his warriors to victory over LaBalme's raiders.

British troops occupied the ruined Miamitown in 1781 before retiring to Detroit.

In the early 1790's two American armies were sent by President Washington to establish a fort at Miamitown. Chief Little Turtle and his forces thwarted these American advances. A third American army under the leadership of General (Mad) Anthony Wayne was sent against the Indians. Little Turtle, realizing this American army was better trained and equipped than the previous American force, refused to join his Indian allies against Wayne. The Indian army under the leadership of Chief Blue Jacket attacked the American forces at a spot approximately 10 miles west of the present city of Toledo, Ohio. This engagement, known as the Battle of Fallen Timbers, was fought in an area where the trees had been blown over by high winds. Wayne's army won a smashing victory over the Indians leading to the establishment of the American military post called Fort Wayne and the founding of the present city by that name.

Five military outposts occupied the three rivers site between 1690 and

1819. The United States Army constructed the last fort on this location in 1815 and 1816. It was garrisoned by American troops from 1816 to 1819. The movement of the frontier west caused it to be abandoned.

Restoration of the 1816 American fort was completed in the middle 1970's. Although it is located approximately a quarter of a mile from its original location the fort has the authenticity of the 1816 military installation.

To enter the fort you must walk over the bridge that spans the St. Mary's River. Here you leave the hustle and bustle of modern life to enter an era of Indiana's history at the beginning of its statehood. The palisaded wood fort has two blockhouses, an enlisted men's barracks, officer's quarters, commanding officer's quarters, hospital, powder room, and storeroom. A museum in the enlisted men's barracks depicts Northern Indiana's history from the ice age to circa 1819. Once inside the fort you will meet people dressed in the clothing of this past era. They will be glad to explain to you what constituted everyday life in the late teens of the 1800's.

The orientation center, which is just before the bridge, has historical publications about the fort and Indiana. An admission is charged to tour the fort.

Historic Fort Wayne is open daily to the public from late April to October. During the months of June through August the hours are 9 to 6, and from 9 to 5 for the months of April, May, September, and October. Persons desiring further information can write to Historic Fort Wayne Incorporated, 107 South Clinton Street, Fort Wayne, Indiana 46802.

To reach Historic Fort Wayne take U. S. Route 30 until it intersects with Indiana Route 27. Turn south on route 27 going toward the downtown area of Fort Wayne. The signs along the highway will guide you to the fort.

Mayes' Corner, Hesston Corners, Hesston - Laporte County

When Matthew Mayes arrived at a rural crossroads in what is now northern Laporte County in 1833 he had no idea what he was going to do for a livelihood. Luckily he was able to obtain employment as a helper in the construction of a sawmill. Over the years Mayes bought a farm and also opened up a blacksmith shop. Mayes' Corner, as it became known, was in the center of a booming lumbering and barrel making area.

P. M. Hess, a native of the State of New York, came to Mayes' Corner in 1856. Hess opened up a store and ran a sawmill on the Galena River. The crossroads became known as Hesston or Hesston Corners. Hess later became a prosperous farmer.

Hesston, which has survived through the years is located at the junction of County Road 1000 North and Fail Road. The hamlet has a restaurant, a general store, a church, and several residences.

If one thinks that this village is typical of other rural hamlets, he is mistaken. The Hesston restaurant has an interstate reputation for its fine food. First time diners smile when they see the outdoor sign of the establishment. It reads: "Hesston Bar; Restaurant And Lounge; State And Madison." It is said, and I know from experience, that if you arrive at the restaurant after 6 P.M. on week ends, you are going to have to stand in line for your meal. The restaurant is open Tuesday through Saturday from 5 to 9 P.M.

Numerous orchards dot the rolling hillsides around Hesston. Visitors can pick, for a charge, in season, fresh peaches, apples, blueberries, cherries, and pears. Antique shops, art galleries, campgrounds, picnic areas, and a ceramic shop can be found in the vicinity of the village. Directions to the orchards and business establishments can be obtained at the Hesston general store or at the restaurant.

The engineer on the Flying Dutchman Railroad's
steam locomotive chats with visitors.

The Laporte County Historical Steam Society operates an outdoor steam museum just to the west of Hesston on County Road 1000 North. Here you can take a ride on the society's two mile railroad line named the "Flying Dutchman." The huffing, puffing, and whistling of the steam engine as it pulls its passenger cars over rolling meadows and through deep forests is a living experience out of America's history. Other steam operated equipment is on display.

If you plan to visit the steam museum you will find it open on week-ends from the end of May to the middle of October. Admission is free except on week-ends when the society sponsors special events, then a modest entrance fee is charged. Information about the Hesston area can also be obtained at the museum.

You can reach Hesston by taking Interstate Route 80 and 90 east out of Gary, Indiana till they junction with Indiana Route 39. Turn north on the state highway till you reach County Road 1000 North. On the northeast side of the intersection there is an old steam locomotive that is used by the steam society as a sign for their museum. Turn east on 1000 North to Hesston.

Interstate Route 94 east out of Gary can also be used to reach Hesston. There is one hitch though, you will have to go over the Michigan state line and take the first interchange south. It will take you south to Indiana Route 39 and County Road 1000 North.

Stockdale
Wabash County

The village of Stockdale is located on the north side of the Eel River just west of the river's confluence with Squirrel Creek. Before the coming of the white man an Indian hamlet called Squirrel Village occupied the site. It was probably named after its headman Chief Squirrel.

Thomas Goudy built a sawmill at this site around 1838. Approximately two years later he built a grist mill. The plat of the town was recorded by Goudy on October 26, 1839. Goudy's new village straddled the Miami-Wabash County Line. Part of it was actually in Miami County.

The first store in the village was established by John Jones in 1848. Four years later a blacksmith shop opened its doors. Stockdale obtained its post office in 1853. It was discontinued in 1882.

A flood hammered the mill doing extensive damage. It was later repaired and put back into operation. In 1857 Baker and Banche rebuilt the mill. Over the years the mill went through a number of owners. In its heyday the mill would grind 1,500 bushels of wheat a month, besides corn and feed. Deliveries of flour from the mill went by wagon to Wabash, Peru, Lincoln, Denver, and Manchester.

The old grist mill at Stockadale.

Stockdale's flourishing mill was the impetus for the continued growth of the town. A second blacksmith shop, a wagon shop, and several general stores opened for business. The Independent Order Of Foresters started its lodge in the town in 1873. A public school and church were built. Ideally, Stockdale's future looked bright.

Two events contributed to the decline of the town. First, the railroad laid its track bed on the south side of the river. Secondly, the establishment and the growth of the village of Roann south of the river, diminished Stockdale's chances for continued progress. By 1884 Stockdale was a shadow of its former self.

The old wooden grist mill, which is on private property, is still standing in Stockdale. An old frame building, that appears to be a former church or school, is located just to the north of the mill across an open field. There are still a number of well kept residences in Stockdale. I was unable to find any operating businesses in the village.

On the south side of the Eel River across from the old mill, the State of Indiana has established a boat launching area. There is a small picnic ground at this site.

To reach Stockdale take Indiana Route 15 north out of Wabash, Indiana until it intersects with Indiana Route 16. Turn west on route 16. It will take you to Stockdale.

Tiptonville
Fulton County

On October 16, 1826, a treaty between the Potawatomie Indians and the United States Government was signed at Paradise Springs, which was located on the opposite side of where the Mississinewa River flows into the Wabash River. The accords called for the Potawatomies to cede much of their territory north of the Wabash River to the United States. In return for this and other grants the Indians were to receive an annual sum of $2,000 for 20 years. The United States was also bound to build a mill on the Tippecanoe River to grist the corn of the Indians. John Tipton, Indian Agent from Fort Wayne was one of the commissioners who signed the treaty.

Commissioner Tipton authorized General Samuel Milroy to build the mill. Milroy felt the best place to build the mill would be on Lake Manitou rather than the Tippecanoe River. Lake Manitou is located at Rochester, Indiana.

The lake's name comes from a Potawatomie word used for both "good spirit" and "evil spirit." Prior to the coming of the white man, the Indians that had hunted and fished this area for over 150 years, believed the lake waters held a monster fish or serpent of supernatural powers.

When the first white man arrived in the vicinity of the present day lake they found five small basins of water, separated by low marshes in most places. At some of these separations between the ponds the ground was high enough for the Potawatomies to farm. Early settlers knew the bodies of water as Devil's Lake.

Preliminary work on the mill started in the spring of 1827. Settlers from Carroll County came over to work on the mill because there were no whites available in the immediate area. General Milroy asked John Tipton whether he could name the mill in honor of him. Tipton assented and the site was christened Tiptonville.

A gray fall afternoon at the Tiptonville mill site.

Construction of the mill was completed in September of 1827. It was a two story frame structure with one run of stones adapted for grinding corn. This was the kind of grain raised by the Indians. A blacksmith shop and homes for the miller and smith were constructed at the site. Sometime later a trading post was established near the mill.

The mill was unable to start immediate operation because the water was too low in the pond. In 1835 the mill ceased operations. This was three years before the removal of the Indians.

A historical plaque marks the former site of Tiptonville. It is on the south side of the dam in Rochester. There is a small picnic ground at the former location of the old town.

Rochester is the county seat of Fulton County. Among the sights to be visited there are the Rochester Depot Museum, the Pioneer Woman's Log Cabin Museum, and the Civic Center Museum. For more information write to the Fulton County Historical Society, 7th and Pontiac, Rochester, Indiana 46975.

U. S. Route 31 and Indiana Routes 25 and 14 converge on Rochester. Once in town take Indiana Route 14 east. When you hit the outskirts of the city there will be a "Y" in the road. The left fork will be route 14. Take the right fork to Lake Manitou and the Tiptonville site.

Waterloo
Dekalb County

Waterloo, formerly Uniontown, is located where the old Fort Wayne, Cold Water, Michigan trail crossed Cedar Creek in Dekalb County. The Miami Indians called the stream "the big red water creek" because of the brown from the many Cedar and Tamarack swamps along its upper course.

One of the first residents in this area was a French fur trader who arrived in the 1820's. He remained there until the beaver were depleted.

Emigration from the east increased the traffic on the trail. In the early

The old William
Spriegel brewery.

1830's the freighters working the trail put pressure on the new county of Dekalb to build a bridge over Cedar Creek. The freighters had great difficulty in fording the stream during times of high water. Newly elected road commissioner Wesly Parks appointed Jim McKay and several others to build the span. When the wooden bridge was ready to be put across the creek a big flood washed it away.

Eventually the dreamed of bridge over Cedar Creek was built. Frederick Krum laid out some housing lots on the 160 acre tract of land he bought near the creek. A general store, a blacksmith shop, and a wagon shop were opened. In 1838 the first doctor started practicing in town. William Spriegel opened up a brewery in 1847.

The village prospered and grew because of the steady emigration of people from the east. At first the little settlement was called Uniontown after the township. In 1844 the United States post office was established. Although the residents of the settlement wanted it called Uniontown the government named the village Dekalb. The name of the village remained Dekalb until 1856 when it was changed to Waterloo.

That same year the railroad arrived in the village. A freight house was built that eventually employed over 125 men. Waterloo remained an important railroad shipping and transfering point through the 1940's.

One of my best sources of information on Waterloo was 95 year old Henry L. Link. Mr. Link remembers the town in its heyday. He considers present day Waterloo a memorial to the past better days of the town.

Waterloo's main thoroughfare, Wayne Street, is lined with buildings out of the nineteenth century. Surprisingly, most of the store fronts are still in use.

The Abbey building which is located on the east side of Wayne Street is one of Waterloo's landmarks. In 1868 Giles T. Abbey saw fit to construct a three story brick business building. This in itself is a rarity because most of the brick structures of the past century were only one or two stories high. Holes upward through the walls of the building, similar to furnace pipes, carried the heat from the fire on the main floor to the upper stories.

Waterloo's old freight station on Lincoln Street is still standing. When you look at the structure it is not hard to imagine that it was once a thriving business operation.

William Spriegel's old brick brewery is located along Cedar Creek in the town. The building, surrounded by dense undergrowth, is inaccessible because it is located on private property. Spriegel started brewing a local beverage known as Spring Water Beer. The brewery was in operation from 1847 to 1877.

You can obtain further information on the town by writing the Waterloo Town Clerk, Waterloo, Indiana 46793.

Waterloo is located on U. S. Route 6, one and one half miles east of its junction with Interstate Route 69.

The Chicago And Wabash Valley Railroad

My Sunday afternoon drive in January, 1974, with my nephew Fred Smith of Hammond, Indiana was very typical of the many weekend journeys we took in the middle 70's. That day, because of our late start, we decided to drive straight south on route U. S. 41 past the Kankakee River and then turn east on some of Newton County's less beaten side roads. We planned to be home by dusk.

This particular Sunday started out bright and sunny. To our dismay, storm clouds gathered in the west, vanquishing the sun from the heavens. We drove along a country road that paralleled the Kankakee River. Luck seemed to be with us as we found what looked to be an old gun club building dating back to the time when the Kankakee Marsh was a hunters paradise. The structure had been remodeled to make several small apartments out of it.

We decided to turn south to catch a road going west to take us back to route 41 because of the dwindling daylight. There was no difficulty in finding one. Coming up to a rural crossroads Fred said, "Stop, Harry. That sign says County Line Road. We could probably take it north over the river."

I replied, "I've never been up that one. Maybe there will be a bridge over the river and then again maybe there won't. We'll find out."

The gravel road at this point had farm land on either side of it. A few miles north the farm land turned into the wooded swamp land that borders the river. We saw an old steel one lane bridge looming up in front of us. A pick-up truck was already on the span coming toward us, making it necessary for me to pull off to the side to wait for him to pass.

Fred and I figured that our new found thoroughfare would bring us out several miles to the east of Lowell, Indiana. As we rounded a slight curve in the road Fred said, "Hey, there's a grain elevator up there."

Sure enough, towering on the northern horizon was an old elevator. I slowed the car for a quick look see around the area. On our right side about a quarter of a mile south of the granary was a small frame house that looked deserted. We stopped a short distance south of the storage bin. Looking to the east across the open farm land we saw a creek running northeast through the field. On the opposite side of the stream there were several old frame buildings. One of them reminded us of a church or school. The other structures appeared to be old one-room houses.

We gawked and talked for several minutes. Fred suggested that it was an old town. I questioned his opinion, but the more I looked at the surrounding buildings, the more I had to agree with him.

Pulling up in front of the old elevator we noticed a commercial nursery just to the south of it. Across the road from us were two substantial brick homes. I said, "Most of the grain elevators that I have seen usually have been on a railroad siding. There's nothing here like that."

Fred shot back, "Not so fast, Harry, Look at that bump in the road. I bet there was a railroad here at one time."

Fred and I returned to the old elevator several times during the next couple of years. On one of these visits I had the pleasant opportunity of talking to a kind woman who lives in one of the brick homes across the road from the granary. She told me that the deserted storage bin was the old Fifield Elevator. I was also told that a man by the name of Benjamin J. Gifford built and operated a railroad that serviced the granary.

With this information, I made a beeline for the library in search of the Gifford railroad. The first thing learned was that the line was called the Chicago and Wabash Valley Railroad. My efforts in researching the subject were rewarding because I found Mr.

The old Fifield Elevator.

Gifford to be an interesting, imaginative, and innovative individual.

Benjamin J. Gifford was born on April 5, 1840 in a log cabin along the Little Rock Creek in Kendall County, Illinois. His parents, Freeman and Comelia Gifford, had migrated westward from the eastern seaboard in 1838. Freeman Gifford took up farming for a livelihood. Ben's mother died when he was six years old. His father later married Lucy Burroughs. Seven children were born out of this second union.

Ben attended Sandy Bluff School located between Sandwich and Plano, Illinois. He worked during the summer to help with the family finances and further his education. Ben became a qualified county school teacher when he was seventeen years old.

Freeman Gifford would take young Ben on the cattle drives to the Chicago Stockyards. Ben developed a keen interest in livestock through these experiences.

One biographical sketch on the life of Benjamin J. Gifford relates that when he was twelve years old he detected the differences in the height of corn grown in dissimilar soils. This spurred Ben on to find out that these differences were caused by the quality of the ground. Ben's early interest in agriculture and raising cattle is credited as being the prime mover in his efforts to drain the swamplands in Illinois and Indiana.

In 1861, when President Lincoln issued his call for volunteers to join the Union Army, Ben joined Company E of the 13th Illinois Volunteer Infantry. Ben was wounded twice in the Battle of Vicksburg. One of these wounds caused a severe injury to his spine. In later years Ben carried a bottle of whiskey in his briefcase to help relieve the pain from the old hurt.

Ben was mustered out of the service after the expiration of his enlistment. He returned to Illinois, formed his own company, and returned to battle until the end of the conflict.

When Ben returned home from the war he married Etta L. Martindale on November 16, 1865. They had a baby boy whom they named Otto. Sadly, young Otto died in infancy.

In the spring of 1868 the Giffords moved from Plano, Illinois to a farm in Champaign County, Illinois. That fall Ben began practicing law in Rantoul, Illinois. He pursued this profession for ten years.

While a practicing attorney Gifford was reportedly at odds with the Illinois Central Railroad over the matter of freight rates. Ben decided to build a competing east-west line named the Havana, Rantoul, and Eastern Railroad. By 1875 Ben had raised $145,000 in subscriptions for the new line. Seventy-five miles of tracks were laid running from Fisher, Illinois to a point near present day Attica, Indiana which Ben called West Lebanon. Jay Gould, one of the nation's leading railroad magnets, bought up the railroad.

Gifford then bought into a New York railroad syndicate that took over the Cleveland and Marietta, Ohio Railroad in 1881. He managed the line for about a year before selling his interest in it.

Ben also began his career as a reclaimer of swamplands in Champaign County. In 1884 he purchased and successfully drained, by a system of thirty miles of ditches, 7,500 acres in that locale. The profit he realized from selling the land enabled him to purchase, drain, and sell the Vermillion swampland in Ford County, Illinois.

It seemed that Benjamin J. Gifford had a penchant for buying and reclaiming swamplands. In July of 1891, he purchased 34,000 acres of marsh land in Jasper and southern Lake Counties, Indiana at an average cost of $4.50 an acre. His next step was to acquire two floating dredges that were kept working until 100 miles of ditches crisscrossed the drying up terrain.

Once the land was reclaimed Ben set out to build houses and barns on some of the divided land parcels. These were put up for sale to the public. A person could purchase a farm from Gifford and pay for it with the profits he netted from the sale of his crops.

In the late 1890's it was estimated that close to a million bushels of corn, oats, onions, and potatoes were grown on the reclaimed land. The prospects for growing larger yields each succeeding year looked bright.

Transportation of the crops to the Chicago market became one of Ben's main concerns. The nearby railroads offered a differential arrangement on shipped goods that made freight rates astronomical. Ben, falling back on his past history of constructing the Havana, Rantoul, and Eastern Railroad, decided that the solution to his problem was again to build his own line. He organized the Chicago and Wabash Valley Railroad on September 10, 1898.

There is a dispute in the written literature of where the railroad actually started. One source stated that Gifford selected a site two miles east of DeMotte, Indiana on the then New York Central Railroad for the base of his operations. He called the site Kersey in honor of one of his nephews by that name. Here Gifford built a depot, granary, general store, school, a shed for his engines, and several houses for his men.

Zadoc, a small hamlet, approximately three and one-half miles south of Kersey is mentioned as the other starting point for Gifford's line. The fact that Gifford maintained the railroad offices in Kersey gives credence to the belief that the railroad actually started there.

In 1901 Gifford had built his railroad south to McCoysburg, Indiana. Here it connected with the Chicago, Indianapolis, and Louisville Railroad, commonly known as the Monon.

The construction of the road in a northerly direction was going on at the same time the line was moving south. Gifford's railroad crossed the Kankakee River at Lake County's southeast corner. From there the tracks were laid to the Fifield Elevator and then up the long since vanished village of Dinwiddie. The Apple Valley Mobile Home Park at Indiana Route 2 and Interstate Route 65 now occupies the former village site.

Gary, Indiana became the goal for the northern terminus of the railroad. By 1912 the line had crept four miles north of Dinwiddie. All construction stopped on the northern stretch of track when Gifford died in 1913.

Before his death Gifford's railroad unexpectedly became a beneficiary of an oil strike in Jasper County. Early in the 1890's a tenant farmer drilling for water for his livestock struck oil. By 1900 there were 100 wells producing 400 gallons of oil a day in the locale of the now extinct town of Asphaltum, Indiana. Gifford, owning most of the leased land, stood to make one-eighth of the profits from the oil field.

Refining equipment was installed in the then thought perpetually oil rich area. The Chicago and Wabash Valley Railroad built a four mile feeder line between the Jasper County towns of Gifford, named after Benjamin J. Gifford, and Asphaltum to service the oil field. Six tank cars were purchased by the railroad. This was the only specialized equipment ever owned by the line.

In 1904, one by one the oil wells started running dry. Refining operations in the Gifford field ceased in September of that year. The spur line remained in place until it was pulled up by the railroad in its 1910-1911 fiscal year.

Clarence Holladay, a retired railroader from Kersey remembers back to 1914 when he started working for the Chicago and Wabash Valley Railroad. On a typical day the locomotive was coaled and fired by 5:30 A.M. It was then backed out of the engine shed and hooked to the waiting passenger coach and box cars. The train would then head south stopping at Zadoc, Laura, Gifford, Newland, and Moody stations to pick up passengers going to McCoysburg to catch the north bound Monon to Chicago. At McCoysburg the Chicago and Wabash Valley train was switched for the trip north up the line to Dinwiddie. The rest of the day would be spent picking up freight like cattle, corn, and eggs.

Holladay stated the train never went faster than 35 miles per hour for fear of derailment. Rain would wash out the dirt under the tracks causing the train to swing sideways. There were a number of derailments owing to the condition of the track bed.

Every fall the farmers would bring tons of potatoes and onions to the little towns along the line. Elevators and some stores were built at these hamlets to service the ever increasing business. The railroad was nicknamed "The Onion Line" because of the large tonnage of vegetables it shipped.

Benjamin J. Gifford suffered a slight stroke on January 11, 1913. His illness extended over a three month period. Mr. Gifford died in the Rensselaer, Indiana hospital on April 9, 1913. Final interment was in Kankakee, Illinois.

The Monon purchased the Chicago and Wabash Valley Railroad after Gifford's death. They operated it as a separate line for two decades. Declining business caused the Monon to curtail its operation of the railroad in the early 1930's. The Interstate Commerce Commission gave the Monon the right to have the Gifford line scrapped in 1936. All that remains of the Onion Line today, is the spur track that runs from the Conrail line to the Kersey elevator.

When Fred and I got the whole story on Benjamin J. Gifford we returned to the Fifield Elevator for a last visit. "No Trespassing" signs had been placed on the premises. Standing on the rural road facing the granary we talked about Gifford and his railroad, I said, "This elevator is a lasting memorial to Gifford."

Fred replied, "You're right Harry, but it may be torn down someday. His real memorial is the farms we can see. As long as the fields are plowed and the crops harvested, Gifford will be remembered."

Many of the small hamlets along the old Chicago and Wabash Valley Railroad right of way are still in existence. To reach Kersey take U. S. Route 231 and Indiana Route 10 east out of DeMotte, Indiana until you see the sign for Kersey. Turn north on the turnoff to Kersey. Gifford and Newland can be reached by Taking Indiana Route 10 east out of DeMotte to its junction with Indiana Route 49. Turn south on route 49 until you see the sign for Gifford. Take the turnoff road west to Gifford. To reach Newland continue south on route 49 past the Gifford turnoff until reaching the sign for Newland. Turn east on the side road to the town.

You can each the old Fifield elevator by taking Indiana Route 2 east out of Lowell, Indiana. When you reach its intersection with Range Line Road turn south. There will be a sign at the crossroads reading "Range Line Church." Follow Range Line Road south to the elevator.

CENTRAL INDIANA

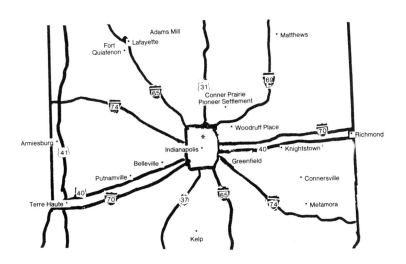

The Miamis

Indiana was named after the American Indians, and rightly so, because numerous tribes over the past centuries have made the territory within the present state boundries their homeland. The Potawatomi, Piankeshaw, Miami, Delaware, Shawnee, Kickapoo, Munsee, Mohegan, and Wea at one time or another resided in the state. An estimated 20,000 Indians lived in Indiana at the time the first European contact was made with them.

History tells us that the Miami Indians were one of the largest and most powerful tribes in North America. At the height of their power in the seventeenth century the Miamis controlled the western part of the State of Ohio, all of the State of Indiana, and the eastern part of the State of Illinois. The chief village and capital, named Ke-ki-o-que in the Miami language, was located where the present city of Fort Wayne now stands.

In the eighteenth century the Miami power started ebbing because of the continuous attacks from hostile tribes. The Potawatomies, occupied Miami land north of the Wabash River. Other Indian tribes, driven west by the pressure of the white man, laid claim to Miami lands located in what is now the central and southern parts of Indiana.

American settlers from the east and the present State of Kentucky started migrating to what is now Indiana in the 1790's and early 1800's. This influx of immigrants caused the United States Congress to establish the Indiana Territory in 1800. The new territory encompassed the present states of Indiana, Illinois, Michigan, Wisconsin, and part of Minnesota.

Virginia born William Henry Harrison was appointed the first governor of the territory. Vincennes was named its capital.

In September of 1802 Governor Harrison negotiated with Indian leaders at Vincennes to settle the boundries of Indian lands near the capital as established by former treaties. This was the first of many treaties Harrison made with the Indians while serving as governor from 1801 to 1812. Each additional treaty added new lands to the dominion of the United States.

British agents started stirring up Indian passions against encroachment of the white man several years before the War of 1812. Two Shawnee brothers, Tecumseh and the Prophet, became leaders of an Indian confederation dedicated to driving the whites out of their land. In 1808 they selected a site for the capital of their confederation along the Wabash River just below its confluence with the Tippecanoe River. They called it Prophet's Town.

Tecumseh's plan was to unite all the Indian tribes east of the Mississippi River against the white expansionism. His mission of unification took him south to the present day southern states in 1811. Before leaving Prophet's Town he issued strict orders to his brother to avoid any conflict with the whites until he returned from his journey.

Governor Harrison, flooded with complaints about the sporadic Indian attacks on the settlements, gathered an army of about 1200 enlisted men and officers at Vincennes to put an end to these depredations. Harrison's army marched northeast toward Prophet's Town. On November 6, 1811, Harrison's forces camped within a few miles of the Indian capital. Harrison sent emisaries to the Prophet asking for a pow-wow the following morning. The Prophet agreed to meet with the governor.

At approximately 4:15 A.M. on November 7, 1811, the Prophet, acting against his brother's wishes, threw his Indian army of approximately 600 warriors against the American encampment. In the ensuing battle the Prophet's army was soundly defeated. According to accounts, 35 Indians died on the field of battle. There has been no estimate of how many Indian wounded were carried off in their retreat. Twenty-five Americans were killed in action. Forty-seven other Americans died from wounds sustained in the conflict or from disease. Most of the Indian depredations against the settlements came to an end until the beginning of the War of 1812.

The United States and Great Britain went to war in June of the above year. Governor Harrison resigned his governorship to command the Northwestern army. Early in the conflict Detroit fell to the British. Fort Dearborn (Chicago) was abandoned by the Americans at the cost of 41 lives.

Harrison wanted to move his army to relieve Fort Wayne which was under seige by the Potawatomies and then continue on to attack Detroit. There was one weakness in this plan - the Miami Indians along the Mississinewa River in present day Wabash County, Indiana. They were unfriendly to the Americans, having been isolated from the whites because of their geographical location. General Harrison feared that the Miamis would supply men and provisions to attack the rear of his army.

Little Turtle, the great Miami chief who had defeated an American militia force commanded by Colonel John Hardin in 1790, and an American army commanded by General Arthur St. Clair in 1791, urged his people not to

*A view of the inside of the Indian Village Church
while it was still an active religious center.*

join Tecumseh and his British allies against the Americans. His death from natural causes at Fort Wayne caused many Miami braves to disregard his words of wisdom.

Chief Metocinyah, another Miami leader friendly to the Americans, urged his Mississinewa Miamis not to join Tecumseh. These pleas, too, fell on deaf ears as his braves deserted him for the lure of war.

Colonel John Campbell, under orders from General Harrison, marched out from Franklinton (Columbus), Ohio with his detachment of 600 men to destroy the Indian villages along the Mississinewa River. The Americans arrived in the river valley on December 17, 1812. They fought a brief engagement with the Indians before destroying three villages.

On the evening of December 17, 1812, Colonel Campbell had his men camp near one of the burned out villages. Early the next morning an Indian band, consisting of about 300 warriors, attacked the American detachment. A fierce battle ensued that lasted over an hour. The Indians, suffering between 30 and 40 killed, broke off the engagement. Eight

Americans were killed and 26 wounded. Colonel Campbell, hearing that Tecumseh was at the head waters of the Mississinewa with a large force, ordered a quick withdrawal back to Ohio. This engagement became known as the Battle of Mississinewa.

The Miamis were under the yoke of the conquering Americans, after the War of 1812 terminated in early 1815. In 1818 they signed the Treaty of St. Mary's. Under its terms the Miamis ceded all their land south of the Wabash River to the United States except the big Miami Reserve. This reserve was an approximate 900 square mile parcel of land lying south of the Wabash River that ran on an east-west line from the mouth of the Eel River to the mouth of the Salomonie River. On a north-south line the reserve ran from the Wabash River to a point 30 miles south of it. Much of the present day Wabash County was included in this reserve.

In 1838 and 1840 special treaties were signed between the Miamis and the United States government. The Indians signed away all the territory they had south of the Wabash River except for a tract of land along the Mississinewa River that was granted to Chief Metocinyah and special grants to individual Indians. Chief Metocinyah's land had a ten mile river front giving the Indians easy access to the river. It became known as the Meshingomesia Reserve, named after Chief Metocinyah's son and successor.

When Chief Metocinyah died in 1840, his son, Meshingomesia, became the last tribal chief of the Miamis in Indiana. The Indians on the reserve, holding their land in common, built their cabins to their own tastes. They didn't pay taxes nor could they be sued because they were wards of the government. Chief Meshingomesia had little to say about the lives of his followers except in the way of advice.

The Indian Village Church located near the southeast end of the reserve was built in the early 1860's by the Indians and white settlers. For many years it had a prosperous Baptist congregation. Chief Meshingomesia was baptized into the church in 1861. He became a faithful member of the congregation. When services were held at the church the men and women sat in opposite sections of the chapel.

Immediately behind the church the Indians selected a site to inter their dead. In later years it became the largest Indian cemetery in Indiana. When Chief Meshingomesia died in 1879 he was buried in the middle of the burial ground. A large monument was erected in his memory.

In the early 1880's the Indians enjoyed a period of prosperity through the sale of their lands and annuities. They used some of their financial gain to erect fine markers over their dead. As the years grew leaner this practice came to a swift halt. The whole western half of the cemetery is filled with unmarked Indian graves.

Just to the east of the church the Indians and whites constructed the Indian Village School. It too, was built in the early 1860's. Chief

Meshingomesia, himself little educated, encouraged the Indian children to get a good education. He could see that the skills of his people would be of little value in the world that the children would live in during their lifetimes.

The Meshingomesia Reserve lasted from 1838 to 1873. Some of the Indians through the influence of unscrupulous whites, became disenchanted with owning the land in common. They pressured Chief Meshingomesia to petition Congress to break up the reserve into individual parcels of land for each member of the tribe. Chief Meshingomesia at first protested, but later gave in to these demands. Congress passed the bill dissolving the reserve in 1873. Unfortunately, much of the individually owned Indian land passed into the hands of greedy land speculators.

Vandals played havoc with the old Indian church and school. Nothing remains of them today. The Indian cemetery also suffered the ravages of the culprits. In recent times Wabash County has assumed responsibility for the care of the cemetery. It has been restored to the limits that are possible under the pre-existing conditions.

To reach the Indian cemetery take Indiana Route 15 south out of Wabash, Indiana. Continue driving south through the small town of LaFontaine. Two miles south of this village, route 15 intersects with County Road 600 North. Turn right, or west, on the county road. You will go over a one lane bridge before you reach the cemetery located on the north side of the thoroughfare. There is a historical marker at the entrance of the burial ground.

Adams Mill
Cutler
Carroll County

John Adams, a relative of Samuel and John Quincy Adams, came to Carroll County, Indiana from Pennsylvania. In 1831 he selected a site on Wildcat Creek to build a sawmill. Adams, with an eye on future business, also built a flour mill during the years of 1835-1836.

In 1837 Boliver Village was platted around the mill. Eight years later, Adams constructed a new four story frame flouring mill that bears his name today. The community around the mill took the name of Wildcat. A post office by that name was established in the mill in 1850. It closed in 1894.

Warren Adams, son of John, ran the mill after 1861. He constructed a home a short ways down the road from the mill in 1870.

On June 25, 1864, The Wildcat Masonic Lodge was organized. It held its meetings on the third floor of the mill until the autumn of 1867. This was one of two known Masonic Lodges in Indiana that had its beginning in a flour mill.

Adams Mill.

The same year Waren Adams constructed his new home the Adams Mill Covered Bridge was built across Wildcat Creek. This move connected the village with other communities in the nearby area. With the coming of electricity Adams Mill for a time turned generators that provided this utility to surrounding communities.

Adams Mill, which is turbine operated, is still operational. A pioneer museum now occupies the premises. Among the exhibits to be seen are an old waterwheel, farm implements and tools from the nineteenth century, and a Connestoga wagon. There is an admission charge to tour the museum.

The Warren Adams house, which is denoted by a sign above the front fence gate, is not open to the public. It is located on the north side of the road just to the west of the mill.

Sadly, the Adams Mill Covered Bridge is closed to traffic. You can still see it by taking the road that runs in a northerly direction on the east of the mill building.

The mill, which is privately owned, is open to the public on week-ends. Tourists sometimes find the mill closed on visiting days. To avoid this difficulty write to the mill to confirm that it will be open on the date you plan to tour the museum. The address is: Adams Mill, Cutler, Indiana 46920.

You can reach Adams Mill by taking Indiana Route 26 east out of Lafayette, Indiana to its junction with Indiana Route 75. Turn north on route 75 until you see signs for Adams Mill and Cutler on the east side of the highway. Follow the Adams Mill signs through the rural village of Cutler to the mill.

Armiesburg
Parke County

Armiesburg located to the west of Rockville, the county seat, has a past that rivals some of the more noted Indiana historical sites. The Big Raccoon, the Little Raccoon, and the Leatherwood creeks pass through

The one room school at Billie Creek Village.

the area on their way to the Wabash River located one and one half miles to the west of the town. This location was ideally suited for commercial development because of these waterways.

The American history of the area began when George Rogers Clark camped there in 1786. General William Henry Harrison's army bivouacked near the mouth of the Big Raccoon Creek in 1811. Harrison's forces marched on to victory when they defeated the Prophet's army in the Battle of Tippecanoe on November 7, 1811.

In 1813 General Samuel Hopkins laid out the first road across Parke County for military purposes. Colonel Zackery Taylor was one of the members of this expedition.

Armiesburg at first was called String-Town because of the way the settlers built their cabins so close together in a long line. Later the name of the village was changed to Armiesburg in honor of the military regiments that camped there.

The village became an important business center in the early history of Parke County. Armiesburg had several stores, a hotel, and a slaughter house.

Enterprising settlers built flatboats on the three creeks and floated them down to the town. Here they would sell them to shippers engaged in transporting produce down river to the southern markets. The selling price for the usual 50 foot by 121 foot flatboat was around $100.00.

During the early 1820's a grist mill was constructed on Big Raccoon Creek. The mill, made out of logs, had a brush dam that fed water into a bucket wheel.

Armiesburg was not without one of Parke County's famous covered bridges. The wooden span crossed Big Raccoon Creek until it was replaced by a two lane concrete bridge in 1917.

Today, Armiesburg is a small rural hamlet consisting of five houses and two trailer homes. There are no commercial business establishments in the village. The hamlet still rates a spot on the Indiana map.

To reach Armiesburg take U. S. Route 36 west out of Rockville for approximately seven miles. Just before you reach the railroad trestle over route 36 there will be a road coming from the south and junctioning with the U. S. highway. Turn left (south) on this county road. It will take you to Armiesburg.

Approximately one mile to the east of Rockville is Billie Creek Village. A highway sign on U. S. Route 36 directs you to its location.

The village is a replica of the small rural communities that existed in the Midwest around the turn of the twentieth century. Most of the buildings that make up the village date back to that time or an earlier period. They were moved from other locations in Parke County to this site.

There are approximately 28 buildings on the 75 acre grounds. Some of the attractions are a one room school house, an old church, general store, newspaper office, blacksmith shop, broom shop, smoke house, and a farm house. Visitors can watch a blacksmith, dressed in the attire of the early 1900's, work his forge, a miller grinding flour and meal, and a seamstress sewing fine seams with her old treadle machine. A wagon ride takes guests down to the farm where they are given an idea of what farm life was like in the 1900 era.

Billie Creek Village is open to the public 12 to 5 Thursday through Sunday from the end of May to the middle of October. For further information write to Billie Creek Village, R. R. 1, Box 6A, Rockville, Indiana 47872. An admission is charged to visit the village.

Connersville
Fayette County

Connersville takes its name from John Conner, one of Indiana's noted pioneers. He came to what is now Indiana around 1802. In 1803 Conner established his first Indian trading post near the present village of Cedar Grove a few miles south of Brookville. Several years later he moved his trading post to where Connersville now stands.

In 1813 Conner recorded the original plat of the town. The vanishing Indian trade was the stimulus needed to motivate Conner into other business enterprises. He established a distillery, sawmill, and grist mill.

Conner distinguished himself as a public servant during his lifetime. He served as a scout and Indian interpreter for General William Henry Harrison, a treaty maker for the pact called the 12 Mile Purchase, a state senator and representative, a member of the commission that selected Indianapolis as the new capitol, and was the first sheriff of Fayette County.

When the Whitewater Canal, which ran from Lawrenceburg to

A sight of the past is glimpsed as this
Whitewater Valley Railroad steam locomotive
leaves a trail of smoke in its wake.

Hagerstown, Indiana, reached Connersville in 1845 the town started on its path to becoming a modern industrialized city. In 1850 there were 70 brick homes, 160 frame buildings, 14 stores, five warehouses, one woolen factory, three grist mills, three sawmills, one oil mill, and the starting of a future bristling buggy manufacturing business.

Shortly after the turn of the century farsighted industrialists started changing over their buggy making businesses to automobile manufacturing. The McFarlan, built in 1909, was the first car manufactured in Connersville. It was followed by the Lexington in 1910. Other autos manufactured in Connersville were the Empire, Van Auken, Kelsey Cycle Car, Howard and Ansted, Auburn, and Cord. At one time Connersville was called the "Little Detroit of Indiana."

Historic Connersville has many interesting places to visit. Some of these are the First Ward Hose House, the Old Elm Farm, the Canal House, and the Reynolds Museum. Every year the Auburn-Cord-Duesenberg Club holds its annual Tour and Meet during the second week-end in June. One of the highlights of this event is a tour through the factory where the cars were manufactured after 1929.

The Whitewater Valley Railroad, Indiana's longest steam operated line, runs from Connersville to Metamora and back from early May to the end of October. It departs from Connersville at 12:01 P.M. each Saturday and Sunday for the one hour and 40 minute trip to Metamora. The train lays over for approximately a hour in Metamora before making the return trip back to Connersville. Passengers riding the train will be following the old towpath of the Whitewater Canal for most of the trip. Tickets for your ride on the Whitewater Valley Railroad (The Canal Route) can be purchased at the station just south of Connersville and east of Indiana Route 121.

For further information on Connersville write to the Connersville Chamber of Commerce, 111 West 7th Street, Connersville, Indiana 47331.

To reach Connersville take Interstate Route 70 or U. S. Route 40 east out of Indianapolis until you reach Indiana Route 1. Turn south on route 1 to Connersville.

Conner Prairie Pioneer Settlement
Hamilton County

William Conner, brother of John Conner, the founder of Connersville, came to what is now the State of Indiana around 1802. Early experiences as youths with the Indians gave the Conner brothers command of several Indian languages. William, like his brother, became a fur trader in what is now Hamilton County. He married a Delaware Indian woman named Mekinges. Six children were born out of this union.

Fur trading proved a profitable business for William Conner. Because of his command of the Indian languages he became a scout and interpreter for General William Henry Harrison. Conner became a successful general merchant and land speculator in later years.

Indian treaties signed in 1818 caused Mekinges and her six children to join her people in their migration west. William gave his Indian family 60 ponies upon their departure. This act, by the standards of that day, made Mekinges and her six children a wealthy family.

In 1820 William married Elizabeth Chapman of Noblesville. Three years

One of the log cabins located at
Conner Prairie Pioneer Village.

later the couple moved into their new two story red brick home located on the top of a bluff that overlooks an ox bow on the White River. Seven children were born out of this union.

The land around the home site became known as Conner Prairie. Conner profitably farmed the surrounding countryside. Upon his death in 1855 the farm passed into the hands of his surviving family.

In 1934 Eli Lilly and his wife purchased the abandoned and run down Conner farm. The Lillys restored the farm and furnished the home in the trappings of Conner's day. As a later date the Lillys bequeathed the Conner farm to Earlham College of Richmond, Indiana.

The college has recreated a rural Indiana village that dates back to circa 1836. There are 25 buildings in the hamlet. Some of the structures, which are log buildings dating back to the nineteenth century, were moved to the site from other areas. Other buildings duplicating the structures of that time were built on the farm. The village includes, besides the log cabins, a number of farm homes, a one room school house, a country store, a blacksmith and pottery complex, and a carpenter's home and shop. Play-acting residents of the village, costumed in the clothes of 1836, enact the daily lives of people in this bygone era.

Conner Prairie Pioneer Village is located just north of Indianapolis on Allisonville Road near Noblesville, Indiana. It is open daily Tuesday through Sunday, April 1 to December 14. For more information write to the Conner Prairie Pioneer Settlement, 13400 Allisonville Road, Noblesville, Indiana 46060. An admission is charged.

Fort Quiatenon
Tippecanoe County

Fort Quiatenon was established by the French in 1717 at a site about six miles southwest of the present city of Lafayette on the Wabash River. The French colonial government was in hopes the military installation would thwart British expansionism into the Wabash and Ohio River regions. Because of its location the fort became an important trading post and a hub for the Catholic Father's efforts to convert the Indians to Christianity.

French voyageurs from Cananda descended the Wabash River each year to trade their goods for the furs trapped by the Indians. Between the years of 1720 and 1760 the settlement grew and prospered. It was estimated during this period between 2,000 and 3,000 French, Indians, and mixed bloods made their home in the vicinity of the fort.

Fort Quiatenon was seized by British Lieutenant Edward Jenkins and his men from Detroit during the French and Indian War (1754-1763.) At first Jenkins and his men maintained good relations with the Indians. As time passed the Indians became riled at the continuing influx of white people moving west, the discontinuance of the French custom of giving gifts, and the high prices the British traders charged for their goods. The seeds of an Indian rebellion were being sown.

Chief Pontiac of the Ottawa tribe became leader of the Indian dissidents. His goal was to drive the whites back across the Appalachian Mountains. Pontiac's forces attacked 12 frontier posts and captured eight of them. Quiatenon fell to Pontiac's warriors when they simply walked into the fort and took Lieutenant Jenkins and his men prisoners on January 1, 1763.

Two French fur traders intervened to save the lives of the British troops. They were later released in an exchange of prisoners in Detroit.

Fort Quiatenon was the site of the settling of Pontiac's Uprising. When British Colonel George Croghan was captured by the Indians he was taken to Fort Quiatenon. Chief Pontiac arrived at the fort in the late summer of 1765. The two leaders conferred about making peace. At the end of these talks Chief Pontiac pulled his tomahawk from his belt and buried its blade into the dirt meaning the end of the hostilities. This act later gave rise to the phrase "bury the hatchet."

Quiatenon was not regarrisoned after the Pontiac Uprising. The settlement remained a small trading and trapping community with a large Indian population. A British agent occupied the post in 1778 while conducting his spying operations against the Americans in the Revolutionary War. He fled for his life when American Captain Leonard Helm occupied the fort for a short time. That same year British Colonel Henry Hamilton with his forces from Detroit stopped at Fort Quiatenon. They were on their way to seize Fort Sackville (Vincennes) from the Americans.

A small French settlement existed around the fort at the close of the American Revolution. The Indians started using the settlement as a staging area for their attacks against the whites. In 1786 the few remaining French settlers had to desert the post because of the increasing Indian hostility toward them.

Fort Quiatenon remained deserted for all practical purposes until its destruction in 1791. General Charles Scott under orders

The blockhouse at Fort Quiatenon Historical Park.

from President George Washington, burned Quiatenon and a number of Indian villages along the Wabash River to the ground.

In 1930 a local physician by the name of Richard D. Wetherill constructed the present blockhouse located at the Fort Quiatenon Historical Park. The mystery of the real location of the old fort wasn't solved until the late 1960's. At that time archaeological excavations revealed the original stockade was approximately one mile down the river from where Dr. Wetherill erected his replica of it.

A visit to the historical park is most rewarding. The blockhouse will give you an idea of how the military installations of those bygone days appeared and were constructed. Visitors to the historical park will find it open to the public from mid April to mid November. There are shelter houses, picnic areas, boat launching facilities, a trading post gift shop, an interpretive museum, and a general recreation area. Persons desiring further information about the historical park should write to the Tippecanoe County Historical Association, 909 South Street, Lafayette, Indiana 47901.

To reach the Fort Quiatenon Historical Park take Indiana Route 43 south through West Lafayette until it intersects with Indiana Route 26. Instead of turning east over the bridge on the combined routes continue driving southwest on South River Road which runs parallel to the Wabash River on its west side. It will take you to Fort Quiatenon.

Kelp
Brown County

Kelp was located in what is now the Brown County State Park. The settlement was first called "Bird's Run Creek." Later the name was changed to Hobbs Creek in honor of one of the early settlers by that name.

Located to the north and west of the old Kelp site is Weed Patch Hill. The origin of this name came from a party of Kentucky hunters who called it that because the summit of the elevation was covered by a thick growth of weeds. Weed Patch Hill is the second highest point in Indiana, being 1,058 feet above sea level. A 100 foot fire tower now graces the summit of the hill.

In 1893 a letter from Washington, D.C. arrived in the Nashville, Indiana Post Office addressed to Postmaster Tom Allison. The correspondence directed Mr. Allison to establish a post office in Hobbs Creek and to recommend a name for it.

While Mr. Allison was reading the letter a young lad by the name of Harry Kelp stopped at the post office. The postmaster favored the Kelp boy, and for lack of a better name recommended in a letter to Washington, that the new post office be called Kelp. Leander Bruce, a land owner in the area, became Kelp's first postmaster.

Approximately 40 families lived along the creek in the vicinity of Kelp. The actual settlement was comprised of several homes and a number of

Strahl Lake in Brown County State Park.

businesses. Besides the post office there was a general store, a school, a Baptist Church, a blacksmith shop, and a sorgham mill.

The residents of Kelp were forced to move from the town when the land was purchased for the Brown County State Park from 1924 to about 1932. At a later date the deserted and crumbling buildings of Kelp were torn down and removed.

The site of Kelp, which is to the south and east of Weed Patch Hill in Brown County State Park is now overgrown with weeds and bushes. There were some foundation ruins of the village still to be found years back, but today, a person could consider himself lucky if he managed to locate any trace of the settlement.

Brown County State Park is known all over the United States for its seasonal beauty. The park, Indiana's largest, covers over 15,543 acres. It was first open to the public in 1929.

Visitors to the park will find facilities for camping, fishing, hiking, and swimming. Saddle horses can be rented or people can bring their own mounts for a ride along the many miles of horse trails. The Abe Martin Lodge and 24 cabins are available for guests who prefer the comforts of home on their vacations. You can obtain more information about Brown County State Park by writing the Department of Natural Resources, Division of State Parks, 616 State Office Building, Indianapolis, Indiana 46204.

Brown County State Park is located on Indiana Routes 46 and 135, just to the east of Nashville, Indiana.

Matthews
Grant County

New Cumberland (Matthews) was laid out in September of 1833 by Robert Sanders as proprietor and Samuel R. Collier as surveyor. Lots were offered for sale in the fall of that year. The first log cabin was constructed at the site around 1836.

In 1840 the first general store opened its doors. A second general store opened up in 1847. Orvill Dennison erected a sawmill in the town in 1848. Five years later he and a partner built a grist mill. A blacksmith shop opened in the village around the same time. The post office under the name of New Cumberland was established on April 1, 1865.

A natural gas belt was discovered in North Central Indiana in the 1890's. Promoters from Indianapolis, with an eye on the potential riches of the new Trenton gas field, quickly purchased over 2,000 acres along the Mississinewa River between Marion and Muncie, Indiana.

The development company platted a new town where the main section of Matthews now stands. One of the development company's directors was Governor Claude Matthews. The new town, known as the "Wonder City," took his name.

Matthews quickly absorbed the small rural village of New Cumberland. On June 25, 1895 New Cumberland's post office was moved "downtown" under the name of Matthews. The combined town had two churches, a steam sawmill, one fraternal lodge, two physicians, and a good school.

All sorts of promotional activities running from multi-colored circulars to bicycle races were used to bring people and industry to Matthews. In 1899

The Cumberland Covered Bridge.

a glass company opened its bottling manufacturing plant in the town. Within a year Matthews had 11 factories producing bottles, window glass, lamp chimneys, and prescription ware. Other plants went into operation producing bricks, lumber products, clay pots for use by the glass industry, and steel products.

In the early 1900's Matthews had an estimated population of over 5,000 people. Housing was so critical a tent city sprang up. The several hotels in the town had people sleeping in the hallways, lobbies, and dining areas. Matthew's taverns, numbering over 20, had no closing hours. The boom, based on the touted unlimited gas supply, was on.

Sadly, nature, the innovator of the boom, lowered the boom on Matthews. By 1905 the "perpetual" gas supply started running out. One by one the factories started closing down or moving to other sections of the country. People knowing the boom was over started drifting to greener pastures. Homes were dismantled and moved to other areas. Bricks taken from the crumbling factory buildings were used to construct homes for the few residents that chose to remain in the vicinity. Matthews, the boom town of over 5,000 people became a ghost town of less than a 1,000 people.

Present day Matthews challenges the imagination to see its former glory. Massachusetts Avenue, the main thoroughfare in town is still lined with old brick and frame buildings. In its heyday, as previously mentioned, Matthews had over 20 taverns, now it has one, and from outward appearances, it is closed.

The town's business district consists of a country store, a pizza parlor, the post office, and the library. One brick building that was formerly a hotel has the upper story windows bricked in. The main street gives to the observant person, the same desolate feelings that you encounter when visiting ghost towns in the west.

On the northeast side of the town you will find the Cumberland Covered Bridge. The span built in 1877, is 181 feet long. In 1913 a flood washed the bridge down stream. It was returned to its original foundation through the use of rollers. The bridge is now on the National Register of Historical Places. You can find the bridge by following the signs in town directing you to it.

To reach Matthews take Indiana Route 26 east out of Fairmount, Indiana to its junction with Indiana Route 221. Turn south on route 221 to Matthews.

Metamora
The Whitewater Canal
Franklin County

Duck Creek Crossing (Metamora) was a small village located on the north side of the Whitewater River in Franklin County. The village got its first post office under the above name in 1826.

In 1838 David Mount and William Holland platted a new town at this site. Mrs. John A. Matson is credited as renaming the village to Metamora. She got the name from a character found in the novel, **Metamora, Beautiful Squaw.** The post office followed suit by changing its name to Metamora during this period.

A number of businesses opened up their doors shortly after the town was platted. Messrs. Churchill and Asa Geltner were the first blacksmiths in the town. David Mount opened up a general store in his home. John McWhorter was the first tavern keeper. John Adair opened up a general store which he later sold to William Holland.

When the Whitewater Canal, which was built between 1836 and

1847, reached Metamora the seed for industrial expansion was planted. A flour mill, woolen mill, wood working factory, and a distillery were opened up in Metamora over the ensuing years.

Metamora's quest for economic progress was doomed by two forces that were the scourge of communities at that time. First, fires plagued the town's industries over the decades. Secondly, time and advancement made water power obsolete.

In 1866 the canal, which for the most part paralleled the Whitewater River, succumbed to the railroads and high cost of maintenance. Most of the canal's 76 miles of right of way between Lawrenceburg and Hagerstown, Indiana was bought up by the competing railroads.

The Whitewater Canal State Memorial preserves 14 miles of the old

The Whitewater Canal State Memorial.

waterway for posterity. Most of the activities center around the restored grist mill located at Lock No. 25 in Metamora. Visitors to the mill can see it in operation grinding wheat into grits and whole wheat flour. While there they can purchase the finished products and visit the museum on the second floor

A person can take a 30 minute cruise along the canal in the Memorial's horse drawn canal boat the "Ben Franklin." Beginning in Metamora the canal trek takes you over the Duck Creek aqueduct, through the Millville lock, and back to town. There is an admission charge for the mill and boat ride.

The restored aqueduct, once featured in Ripley's "Believe It Or Not," carries the canal boat 16 feet above Duck Creek. It is 80 feet long and believed to be the only such structure in existence.

Located near Laurel, Indiana is the Laurel Feeder Dam, where water from the Whitewater River is channeled into the canal. Fishing, tent sites, and picnic areas are available at the feeder dam. Picnic areas are also available at the Millville lock and the grist mill.

The mill is open daily from 9 to 5, except in the winter months when it is on a five day a week schedule. Visitors can board the "Ben Franklin" on week-ends and holidays from May 1 to October 31. For more information on the Whitewater State Memorial write the Division of Museums and Memorials, Department of Natural Resources, 202 North Alabama Street, Indianapolis, Indiana 46204.

Metamora is serviced by the Whitewater Valley Railroad. Details about the steam operated line are given in our Connersville listing.

Numerous antique, craft, and souvenir shops await your visit to Metamora. Many of these shops are located in the antiquated buildings of the town.

Metamora is located on U. S. Route 52 approximately 60 miles southeast of Indianapolis.

Woodruff Place
Indianapolis
Marion County

James O. Woodruff laid out Woodruff Place in 1872 and 1873. He intended to create an exclusive suburban town outside of the noise and distraction of Indianapolis. Woodruff was financially ruined in the Panic of 1873, but the community carried on his name. Woodruff Place was incorporated in 1876.

The town had three north-south well shaded boulevard drives bisected by grassy esplanades. Statuary animals and water fountains were placed in these open places.

Just after the turn of the twentieth century Woodruff Place had established itself as a wealthy and affluent community. The alleys between the north-south drives were lined with carriage houses and servant quarters. Some of the more prominent citizenry in the town were Charles E. Test, president of the National Motor Company, Rear Admiral George Brown, a retired naval officer, Chauncey Butler, the son of educator Ovid

Butler, Brandt T. Steele, son of famed Indiana artist T. C. Steele, and William H. Hart, state auditor during the 1890's. The modest homes of the less affluent were built on the smaller lots in the community.

By the 1920's Woodruff Place was surrounded by Indianapolis on all sides. The slow paced existence and tranquility that characterized the town disappeared as the noise and the fast paced life of the big city enveloped the community. Some of the wealthy residents moved to other suburban areas to regain the quiet life.

The depression of the 1930's reduced the number of people who

*One of the street water fountains
found in Woodruff Place.*

could keep up the huge residences. Many of the homes were divided up into small apartments. This trend continued when the returning World War II servicemen sought places to live.

Woodruff Place survived as a separate community until 1962. Soaring police and fire protection costs forced the community to merge with Indianapolis.

The Woodruff Place Civic League is now hard at work to preserve the community's heritage. Several plush homes have been purchased by families and individuals dedicated to restoring them.

One of the most interesting structures in Woodruff Place is located at 608 Middle Drive. This 28 room, three story Victorian dwelling, complete with elevator, once served as a sanatorium. Dr. Fremont Swain, M.D., O.D., and Dr. Rachael Swain, M.D. encouraged people suffering from any number of diseases to visit the sanatorium with its clean air and healthy environment. What cures were effected is not known.

The sanatorium fell is disrepair in the early 1950's. In March of 1975 the building was sold to a family interested in restoring it. This home has been open to scheduled public tours.

Woodruff Place is located between 10th Street and Michigan Street on Indianapolis' east side. Visitors interested in taking scheduled public tours of the homes should write to the Woodruff Place Civic League, Inc., 720 West Drive, Woodruff Place, Indianapolis, Indiana 46201.

To reach Woodruff Place take Interstate Route 70 east past the Weir Cook Airport. Continue on Route 70 through the center of Indianapolis. Keep an eye open for the Rural Street Exit. Turn south on Rural Street until it intersects with 10th Street. Turn west on 10th Street to Woodruff Place. It will be on the south side of the street just before you reach the Arsenal Technical High School.

Four Towns Along The Old National Road

In November of 1753, a party of seven Englishmen bundled up against the winter cold, rode single file out of Cumberland, Maryland, bound for a French fort said to be located at the mouth of the Monongahela River in the then disputed territory of what is now the State of Pennsylvania. Behind the party's scout Christopher Gest, rode a 20 year old major named George Washington. The party's mission was to deliver dispatches from Virginia's Governor Robert Dinwiddie to the French commandant, stating Virginia was laying claim to the Ohio Country which later became the Northwest Territory.

Washington saw at that time the need of a road to tie the Eastern seaboard states with the developing west. Early in the French and Indian War (1754-1763) Washington and his troops cut a military trail through the forests that followed the general route of the future National Road.

When Washington became president he continued advocating the construction of such a road, but it wasn't until after his death that his dream started becoming reality. In 1806 President Thomas Jefferson signed a bill authorizing the construction of the first leg of Washington's dream between Cumberland, Maryland and Wheeling, West Virginia. Five years later the actual construction of the road commenced. Eventually, the road would stretch from Cumberland to St. Louis, Missouri.

In 1827 a Federal survey party led by Jonathon Knight started laying out the National Road in Indiana. Plans called for the road to be 80 feet wide with the center 30 feet to be covered with graded stone for mail and passenger coaches.

Construction of the Indiana segment of the National Road began in 1829 and was completed in 1834. From the start the road was clogged with people walking, Conestoga wagons, stage coaches, mail coaches, carriages, hand drawn carts, hand push carts, and anything beyond description that had wheels on it. People were moving to Indiana and beyond.

Towns sprang up along the road to service the ever increasing traffic. Many of them started with a tavern, hotel, general store, and blacksmith

Putnamville's post office with an abandoned residence in the background.

shop. Some of these were Pershing, Cambridge City, Knightstown, Greenfield, Belleville, Stilesville, Putnamville, and Brazil.

The old National Road became the new U. S. Route 40 in 1925. By 1935 route 40 was widened to become a major east-west coast to coast highway. The decade of the 1960's saw the decline of route 40 when it was replaced by the Interstate System. In 1976 the National Road was declared a National Historic Civil Engineering Landmark.

When towns are bypassed by a newly constructed highway they merely become dots on a map to the scurrying cross state travelers. What these towns are today and what they were in the past is actually a story written by the local populace and a story that should be told.

My wife Marilyn, grandson Jamie, and I took a trip down memory lane when we decided to include the old National Road in this book. We found time has dealt harshly with some towns while it has been great with other ones.

The first town we visited was Putnamville. It is located at the junction of U. S. Route 40 and Indiana Route 243 in Putnam County. Putnamville's business district consists of a country store, a Methodist church, post office, and an abandoned business building.

We parked on the south side of route 40 to take pictures. Looking around, we saw that the church off to the south of us, was sitting on a slight ridge some distance from the road. It had a huge front lawn that ended at a two foot high concrete wall running along the front of the property facing the highway. In the wall we found a set of concrete steps going up to the

An antique shop located on the old
National Road in Belleville.

lawn. There was no pathway leading back to the church. We speculated that at one time the concrete stairs either led up to a business establishment or a private home.

Our drive through the village only took a few minutes. We found the homes neat and well kept.

Putnamville's history goes back to 1830 when James Townsend laid out the town on land that was purchased from Edward Heath. The alleys of the new community were to be six feet wide and the streets 60 feet wide.

The town grew rapidly with the coming of the National Road. Because of its location and progress there was agitation in the county to move the county seat from Greencastle to Putnamville. The move floundered because the necessary political strength could not be mustered.

When the question came up of where to locate the Methodist college (DePauw University) in Indiana, Putnamville was again Greencastle's rival. Other competitors for the site were Indianapolis, Rockville, Lafayette, and Madison. Putnamville was so sure they would get the college the town fathers laid out a location for it and named the street running to the proposed campus, College. The college site went to Greencastle when they underbid Putnamville by $5,000. This second loss, at the hands of Greencastle seemed to stunt Putnamville's growth for a number of years.

In 1832 Putnamville had a blacksmith shop, a harness shop, wagon shop, shoe shop, and a hotel. The saw and grist mills were located on the outskirts of the town. By 1864 there were more than 50 buildings in Putnamville. Besides the usual frontier shops, the town had added a school on the public square and three churches. Several years later the town got a newspaper called the "Putnamville Philomatheon Times."

Putnamville continued to be plagued by bad luck. In the late 1870's a disastrous fire broke out in the town that destroyed several business establishments, the public library, and the post office. It is said the town never completely recovered from the inferno.

The next town we stopped at was Belleville in Hendricks County located at the junction of U. S. Route 40 and Indiana Route 39. Most of the town's businesses front along route 40. Besides the normal commercial establishments the town has two antique stores, a seasonal produce market, a woodworking shop, and a variety store.

James Whitcomb Riley's boyhood home.

Once off the busy highway the small rural village atmosphere cannot be missed. The homes of the community are in excellent condition.

Belleville's history begins in 1829 when William Hinton, Lazarus Wilson, and Obediah Harris laid out the town. Hinton built the first house and store within the village limits. The post office was established in Belleville on Dec. 29, 1831. Milton W. Hensley was named the first postmaster.

The town experienced constant growth because of the ever increasing traffic along the National Road. By the 1840's Belleville had five or six inns, three blacksmith shops, two general stores, a drug store, two cabinet shops, a cradle (reaping) factory, two cooper's shops, a sawmill, a grist mill, a woolen shop, a planing shop, a gun shop, and a combined blacksmith and buggy shop. By virtue of this progress Belleville became one of the county's main commercial centers.

In 1850 the railroad bypassed Belleville when it laid its road bed to the north of the town. This move stifled and even reversed Belleville's economic progress.

Belleville was destined to experience another era of progress with the coming of the automobile. When route 40 was made into a major coast to coast highway the heavy traffic along this artery was a boon to Belleville's economy. Truckers made it a habit to eat in the town's restaurants.

Sadly, the Interstate highway system brought an end to Belleville's new found wealth.

We passed through Indianapolis on our way to visit the eastern half of Indiana's old National Road. Our destination was Greenfield, Indiana, located at the junction of U. S. Route 40 and Indiana Route 9.

Being centrally located, Greenfield became the county seat of Hancock County. It is a bustling and progressive town. Commercial enterprises abound in the community. The new residential areas in and around Greenfield leave little doubt that this area is on the move.

In 1850 Greenfield had 300 residents. Today, over 10,000 people live in the town.

Greenfield was first settled by Meek and Spillman in 1828. Thirty years later the town consisted of the county courthouse, county offices, county seminary, several business establishments, and 60 residences.

The famed Hoosier poet, James Whitcomb Riley, spent his childhood years in a home located on West Main Street (route 40) in Greenfield. Reuben Riley, father of James, was a carpenter and an attorney-at-law. He built the 10 room, Italianate styled frame house in 1850.

James was approximately two years old when he and his family moved into their new home. He spent the next 20 years watching people migrating west along the National Road.

Riley's boyhood home has been restored and is now a museum. It houses memorabilia that he collected during his lifetime. The home is open for public viewing 10 to 5 Monday through Saturday, and 1 to 5 on Sunday, May through October. There is an admission charge.

For further information write to the James Whitcomb Riley Home, 250 West Main Street, Greenfield, Indiana 46140.

Twelve miles east of Greenfield is Knightstown, located at the junction of U. S. Route 40 and Indiana Route 109 in Henry County. To our surprise, we found a thriving community. The business section of the town lines route 40 and extends down some of the side streets. It seemed to us the old Knightstown Hotel (circa 1860), located on the north side of route 40 between North Washington and North Adams, was waiting for us to take its picture.

The old Knightstown Hotel.

We found several historic buildings dating back to the latter half of the 1800's on our drive through the busy but pleasant town. Among these were the Alhambra Theatre (circa 1897), the Knightstown Academy (circa 1877), and the Mills House (circa 1864).

To find these buildings start at the junction of North Washington and route 40. Turn north on Washington until you reach the middle of the first block. The Alhambra Theatre is located near the center of this block on the east side of the street. Continue driving north on Washington until it intersects with Penn Street. The Knightstown Academy will be on your right side (east) as you approach this intersection. Turn east on Penn Street for one block to its junction with North Adams. Turn south on North Adams. Near the end of the first block on the east side of the street you will find the Mills House.

Waitsell M. Cary platted Knightstown in 1827. He purchased the land on which the town now stands when the National Road was being surveyed. As you might have expected, the village was named Knightstown, in honor of Jonathan Knight the chief government surveyor.

In 1829, Isaac Jones and Levi Griffith in partnership, opened the first store in the town. Waitsell Cary opened a licensed tavern in 1832 that provided food and entertainment to people traveling the National Road. Knightstown opened its post office in January of 1833.

The new village at first grew slowly. One historian wrote that the amount of fighting and whiskey drinking was large in proportion to the population. It is stated that even after 1830 bears were sometimes seen in the streets of Knightstown.

In 1865 the Soldiers and Seamen's Home was opened up two miles south of Knightstown. The following year saw the opening of the Soldiers Orphan's Home. Today, these facilities are named the Indiana Soldiers and Sailors Children's Home. It is not open to the public.

Knightstown in later years became an important trading point. One of the main contributors to this success was the Chicago, St. Louis, and Pittsburg Railroad which ran through the community.

In 1850 Knightstown had a population of 700 people. Today, an estimated 2,600 people live in the community.

Our trip along the old National Road was a complete success for us. We were able to gain a new respect for indiana's past and a greater appreciation of our state as we know it today. It is our hope, that you too, will travel along, "Indiana's Highway Of History."

SOUTHERN INDIANA

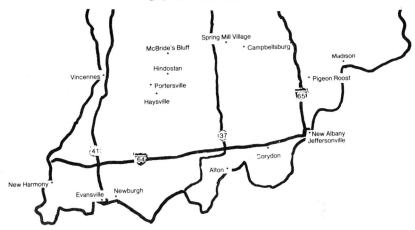

The Lost Indian Treasure Cave of McBride's Bluff

One of the most fascinating Indiana treasure tales is the lost Indian treasure cave of McBride's Bluff. The bluff is located in Martin County, approximately four miles northeast of the town of Shoals on the east fork of the White River. In some places the sandstone cliff is sheer-faced and rises as high as 200 feet above the water level.

Early in the 1950's a tattered, wrinkled, gray-headed old man, wearing what looked to be a World War I overcoat, paid a visit to Mrs. Ruby Stiles of Shoals. Mrs. Stiles was past president of the Martin County Historical Society. The elderly man's name was W. H. McBride.

He was a descendant of an early pioneer family by that name that settled in Martin County. McBride gave Mrs. Stiles a 10-page typewritten manuscript titled "Story of the Silver Bricks." Strangely, McBride listed Mrs. Stiles and himself as co-authors on the title page. Mrs. Stiles adamantly denied having anything to do with McBride's literary 'endeavors. Some people say McBride used her name to lend prestige to the story.

According to the story, one of the first settlers in Martin County was a man named Absolum Fields, who built his cabin in Mitcheltree Twp. near the east fork of the White River. One evening when Fields was out calling his horse he was approached by three laughing Indians. One of them told Fields in broken English not to be scared, but they were going to make him go see something and then bring him back to his cabin.

The Indians blindfolded Fields and tied his hands behind his back. After

— 59 —

they turned him around several times, the Indians made him walk in an unknown direction. Then Fields was placed in a boat and paddled some distance before it landed. The Indians made Fields walk in another circle before they led him into what he thought was an underground passageway.

When the blindfold was taken off, Fields found himself in a cave with Indian women and children. The Indian braves showed Fields some small metal bricks which they said were silver. He was then shown the place where they had mined the ore.

Fields again had his hands tied behind his back, was blindfolded, and returned to the boat. On the return trip Fields tried to figure out whether he was going up or down river. His sense of direction was completely lost. As they had promised, the Indians returned Fields back to his cabin unharmed.

Some time after this, the Indians on McBride's Bluff, who were thought to be Choctaw, fought a running battle with the soldiers from Fort Ritner, Indiana. The Indians were overwhelmed and forced to flee the area. Before they left, the Indians sealed the entrance to the treasure cave with rocks, trees, and brush.

Many years later Absolum Fields contracted out to work on a flatboat carrying farm produce down the White, Wabash, Ohio and Mississippi rivers to New Orleans. While on this trip south, Fields bumped into a Choctaw. When the Indian found out Fields was from Martin County he told him, "If white man only knew, could shoe horse with silver cheap as iron."

Fields, recalling the cave he had been shown by the Indians, prodded the Choctaw for more information. The Indian indifferently said, "You stand on

The pioneer cemetery on top of McBride's Bluff.

big bluff, look way over in big bottom, maybe it over there, maybe not. Look up river, maybe up there, maybe not. Look down river, maybe down there, maybe not."

"Look way in toward medicine waters, maybe over there, maybe not. White man heap big fool, never find, dig till most to it, then he quit."

Try as Fields may, he was unable to get more information from the Indian. When Fields returned to Martin County he spent all his spare time looking for the treasure cave.

Fields remembered the silver bricks as being three to four inches wide on the broad face, but not quite so wide as the other end because they had been cast in a flaring mold. The silver bars were from three to eight inches long, and from one-half to three-quarters of an inch thick.

McBride wrote that he had seen two such metal bricks found by Lonzo Marley on his farm along Indian Creek, north of Trinity Springs, Indiana. Marley plowed up one brick and found another at an old Indian ford when the water was low.

One brick was six inches long, three inches wide, and one-half inch thick. The other was eight inches long, four inches wide, and three-quarters of an inch thick.

Marley had both bricks assayed in 1909. They were 80 percent silver. McBride claims to have seen the assay reports.

According to McBride, one day in 1909, seven young Indians got off the train in Shoals, walked west across the railroad bridge over the east fork of the White River and headed northeast toward McBride's Bluff. Some of the local citizens tried to follow the Indians, but quickly lost their trail.

Several days later, the Indians were again seen crossing the railroad bridge going toward the railroad depot. Two of the Indians were carrying a long pole between them with a blanket tied to it. They boarded the train and were never seen again. It was surmised by the citizens of Shoals at that time that the Indians went to McBride's Bluff, obtained some silver, and departed for parts unknown.

Another source for the above story is in the book, "History of Martin County," by Harry Q. Holt. His version of the tale almost duplicates the manuscript given to Mrs. Stiles by W. H. McBride.

U. S. Geological Survey maps indicate that the gravel road at the foot of the bluff ran only part way along it. New construction has now extended the roadway the complete length of the bluff.

The map showed an old graveyard on top of the bluff. It was named McBride Cemetery, named either for the McBride family or after the name of the bluff.

In August of 1971 my wife, Marilyn, and I made our first visit to McBride's Bluff. We started at the north end of the bluff and drove south on the single-lane gravel road that runs at the foot of the cliff parallel with the White River. The trees seemed to grow right out of the sandstone. In some spots the underbrush at the foot of the bluff was almost impenetrable. When the trees thinned out we could see the sheer face of the bluff rising high above the road.

A short distance down the road we ran into a group of cabins. Some of them appeared not to have been lived in for quite some time.

Continuing down the roadway we found an abandoned old bus near the base of the bluff. The wheels had been removed and the vehicle sat on the ground. All the windows had been broken out of it. Camp gear was strewn all about the interior of the bus.

Marilyn spotted two other makeshift shelters. Later on we found out they were probably thrown up by fishermen that frequented this stretch of the river.

We found a cave whose entrance was almost a half circle. Water running off the top of the bluff showered down in front of the cave. We also noticed water trickling out of the cavern and running down the side of the bluff. In order to explore the passageway one would have to start on his hands and knees and eventually end up crawling through water on his stomach. Cave spelunking was not earmarked for this trip.

Our efforts to find the cemetery on top of the bluff were unsuccessful.

I returned to McBride's Bluff several times during the ensuing years. On one visit my nephew Fred Smith, friend John Grzeczka, and I discovered and explored a second cave along the bluff. This cavern had a natural entrance that required one to bend over to enter it.

A few feet inside the cave someone had seen fit to dig a tunnel into the side of the bluff. The natural passageway became an up and down rectangular shaft with even sides, ceilings and floor. We walked hunched over through the tunnel until we found a pile of rocks and dirt that blocked our way. At the top of this stack of debris was a natural opening, but too small for any one of us to pass through.

Also just inside the cave entrance was a small side cavern. It ran perpendicular to the main entrance. I managed to crawl through the small opening, but not without some difficulty. The passage was mostly a belly-crawling one. In some spots you could get up on your hands and knees.

Using my flashlight, I explored about 60 feet of passageway. When it seemed to be getting smaller I managed to get myself turned around and crawled back to the entrance.

None of the local people we talked to could explain the man-made tunnel we had discovered. It was news to them.

We were in luck this trip as we found the McBride Cemetery on the top of the bluff. It was located in the middle of the woods. Trees and underbrush grew in abundance among many of the gravestones. The older tombstones were sandstone slabs, but a few granite headstones were interspersed among them. We suspected that the newer tombstones were put there by the descendants of the deceased to replace the older, crumbling, sandstone slabs.

The last person buried in the McBride Cemetery, as far as we could discover, was interred in 1888.

We did not find the name McBride inscribed on any of the markers. This led us to believe that the cemetery got its name from the bluff and not because it was a McBride family burial plot.

In some places in the cemetery we found small sandstone slabs just barely sticking out of the ground. There were no inscriptions on any of them.

Why the Martin County pioneers decided to bury their dead on top of McBride's Bluff, far from any known church or town, remains a mystery to us. One local person told me that the Indians started burying their dead on the bluff and the early settlers simply followed suit. If this is true the small, unidentified sandstone slabs could be markers for the Indian dead.

A group of men reportedly from Chicago and Detroit combined their efforts to launch an extensive search for the McBride treasure cave. How they selected the site for their dig remains a matter of dispute.

One version of the story tells of the group chartering an airplane outfitted with special cameras to photograph the bluff. To their surprise, one picture showed an ornamental casket partially buried in the bluff. The burial box had vertical spiral arms extending up at each corner of it. One of these arms had broken away from the coffin.

The second tale has the group hiring a man with a dousing rod to find the treasure site. He was able to locate an area on the bluff where there was a strong pull on the rod. The douser claimed that was the place where the hidden cave was located.

Whatever means they used to select a site, the out-of-state group actually hired a Shoals contractor to dig up the bonanza on McBride's Bluff. Financial difficulties forced the operation to shut down as the hole that they started yielded only dirt and rock.

When the Chicago and Detroit men left for home they reportedly vowed to return with more funds to resume their digging. Their reported vow seems to be empty words; as of yet, they have not returned.

Western treasure legends have dominated the American scene for the last century or more. Recently the eastern half of our country has been awakening to the fact that it, too, has much to offer in the treasure lore field. Indiana residents can actively participate in this renaissance if they desire, as there are many little known tales referring to general locations of lost treasure in the Hoosier state, such as the intriguing story of McBride's Bluff.

Indiana's Silver Rush
Of The 1880's

In the 1880's Indiana experienced a silver rush. It occurred at Buck Shoals, on the east fork of the White River in Dubois County three miles east of Haysville, on property now owned by Mr. and Mrs. Leander Hacker.

Buck Shoals played a major role in the lives of the Indians and early pioneers in the area. Here hunters could hide amid the rocks and wait for deer and elk to wade across the shoals on their way to the valley below.

The Indians are credited with originating tales of silver at Buck Shoals, which were picked up by early settlers. But it wasn't until the 1880s that anyone took a serious interest in them.

Then, suddenly something set off the silver rush. Whether or not any silver was involved still is a matter of dispute. Nonetheless, the rush was on.

Around the time of the silver "find," or shortly thereafter, two strangers, Prof. Hartsfeld and Prof. Brooks, appeared on the scene. They liked to be called the two "Forty-niners."

Prof. Hartsfeld was in the business of selling ore smelters under the name of "Hartsfeld Patented Smelting Furnaces." A St. Louis, Mo., firm, the National Ore and Reduction Co., owned and produced the smelters.

The "professors" and John Seitz of Haysville formed a business alliance and called it the Buck Shoals Mining and Smelting Co. Seitz became president of the firm and a heavy investor in it.

Mr. and Mrs. Jacob Nenkan owned the land where the supposed silver strike was made. They too, became heavy investors.

Before long a 20-ton Hartsfeld Smelter arrived at Haysville and was erected. Though most were given the idea the smelter was for silver production, few, if any realized it was an iron ore smelter and there was iron ore in the area.

But despite this, silver excitement continued to spread in Haysville. Plans were made to build a railroad along the White River to connect the community with Indianapolis, Cincinnati, and St. Louis. Lots were laid out to attract settlers to the town. Haysville was on its way to becoming a boom town.

One of the sale bills for lots in the community read in part:

"Great Sale Of Lots in the town of Haysville, Dubois County, Indiana, Wednesday, February 15, 1886.

"Located eight miles from Jasper, the county seat, Haysville is on the East Fork of the White River, which is navigable a good portion of the year, one mile from the famous Buck Shoals Mining Camp, and is surrounded by veins of excellent bituminous coal, which makes fine coke, a new bridge will soon be erected to connect the North and South bottoms and bring a large trading population to the place and the erection of a roller process flouring mill will draw the trade of a large territory to this place which now go more than double the distance to get their milling done.

"A railroad is surveyed up the White River which will bring the town in direct communication with Indianapolis, St. Louis, Evansville, and Cincinnati. The surrounding county abounds in one timber, and is one of the best wheat producing sections in the state. Now is the time to buy and catch the boom, which is sure to follow in the wake of the many improvements that are to be made immediately. Title perfect. Warranty deeds given. Terms of Sale: One half cash, Balance in one year, with 6 percent interest from the date of the sale."

The boom that circular described really never got off the ground. A report that the cost of reclaiming the silver would exceed the market value of the processed metal helped quell the silver excitement. The smelter closed down. The company was dissolved, leaving its financial backers holding the bag. Part of the smelter still stands as a memorial to the big splash.

Many have wondered how the Haysville silver rush got started. True, the Indians are given credit for originating the silver legend.

Some tales say the Indians had secret lead mines, but could not reveal these sites to the white man for fear of having their tongues cut out.

Indiana pioneers are said to have mined lead, but they, too, were supposed to have kept a tight lip about the sources. What mystifies some is the fact that the names of the white miners never were recorded.

Harry Holt in his work titled, "The History of Martin County" mentions tales of lead deposits in the hills of that area. Such tales still are prevalent.

The patriotically painted old Haysville metal smelter.

When native lead is found it usually contains a little silver and antimony, and is usually associated with zinc. If lead had been found in the Haysville area, there also was a chance that some silver might exist. But today not even lead has been found.

The source for most of the lead and silver tales in Indiana probably is the smattering of the mineral "galena" that dots the state. Galena is an important source of lead.

Most authorities believe that the small galena nuggets found in Indiana were dropped off during the glacial times when huge masses of ice retreated northward. Some of the galena might have come from the Illinois, Iowa, and Wisconsin lead-zinc area via trade among the Indians.

Galena is a heavy, brittle, silver-gray mineral which commonly forms cubic crystals. When broken up, galena has a shiny metallic appearance that at times has been mistaken for silver.

Slag iron and galena have been found at the site of the smelter at

Haysville. The galena probably was brought in along with fluorite from Hardin County, Illinois, for operation of the iron smelter. Fluorite is used as a flux in smelting iron ore and in the production of glass.

Apparently the chunks of fluorite were hand crushed. When they contained too much galena they were tossed aside.

So the silver rush might have been started by someone who broke open one of these chunks of imported galena and thought it was silver. The word spread like wild fire in the area and overnight these rumors changed the iron smelter into a silver smelter.

Another unusual aspect of the Hoosier "silver strike" was a dispute concering the location of the ore. Some said the silver was taken from the river bottom, others claim the silver was mined across the river, and still another story establishes the silver mine up river.

In the Fall of 1975, Indiana's state geologist, Dr. John B. Patton, and Julius Buettner of the DuBois County Historical Society visited the Haysville smelter site. Buettner found a spot on the ground that appeared to contain intermixed gravel and coal ashes. Using his chipping hammer he dug up a piece of galena.

Buettner and Patton agreed the evidence indicated galena found in the area was not from the Haysville area, but probably had been shipped in with fluorite from Hardin County, Illinois.

There were reports that a coal mine had been located in the vicinity of the iron smelter, but no evidence of this could be found. Back at the Hackers was a ladle that had been used at the smelter. It was a bell shaped affair with the open end up. It couldn't have been much more that two feet deep.

Hacker also displayed a huge piece of slag iron in the shape of a halved apple. It weighed well over 200 pounds. Apparently this slag iron had come out of the ladle.

So apparently, the Haysville silver rush resulted from the operations at the old iron smelter. Clay ironstone ores were available in the Haysville area or could have been shipped down the White River from Martin County, IN. Coal supplies were available for the making of iron, as this region is steeped in coal. Fluorite used as a smelting iron flux was probably shipped, along with galena, from Illinois. All these ingredients add up to the processing of iron. The slag iron near the smelter offers proof of this. However, there still are some in the Haysville area who dispute this, although they are unable to agree where the silver ore was mined. The silver processing activities at Haysville were said to be curtailed because of cost and not because the mineral was exhausted. If there is silver in the vicinity of this community, it has yet to be re-discovered. The geology of the area casts doubt on this possibility, but as long as man has an imagination, the Haysville silver story will live on.

Alton
Crawford County

The drive to Alton is one that all flatland Hoosiers will remember. A hardtop road from Beechwood, Indiana takes you south through the rolling hills till you reach the descent into the Ohio River Valley. The downhill drive, with its dodging of chuck holes, following of slow moving farm vehicles, and numerous curves is a real adventure. Nature's beauty is at its best along the winding road.

Alton was founded in 1835. It is located on the Ohio River in Crawford County approximately two miles east of the Perry County line. The town is situated along the river bank. In the middle 1800's Alton was a busy river port. There were two churches, several residences, and a number of business establishments. The Indiana Oak Mills were located at the mouth

One of the Alton's prosperous river boat captains
built his home in the likes of his steamship.

of the Blue River on the edge of the town. At one time it was the largest manufacturer in the county.

Approximately six miles from Alton is the former site of the White Sulphur Well. Wildcatters sinking a well for petroleum struck a pool of sulphur water. This find was instrumental in the starting of a health resort at the location. It was believed that the mineral water had unexcelled medicinal properties. A hotel and dance hall were constructed at the site. Every year throngs of people would travel to the sulphur well for cures of their ailments and for continued good health. Some people believe that the White Sulphur Well took its name from the then well known White Sulphur Springs of Virginia.

Today's Alton has only one business establishment. It is a combination gasoline station and general store. Some residences, but fewer in number as compared to Alton's heyday, still line the river. Power lines that once fed into a vacation trailer park are in disrepair. A church that still appears to be in use sends up its spire above the surrounding houses. The pleasure boat ramp leading down to the river is the only sign of any marine activity. One river boat captain saw fit to build his residence in the shape of his steam boat. The house is still occupied and sits on a high ridge on the northern limits of the town.

To reach Alton take Interstate 64 west out of New Albany to its junction with Indiana Route 66. Turn south on route 66 till you reach its junction with Indiana Route 62. Go west on route 62 until you reach the small town of Beechwood. When you reach the general store in town there is a junction with a hardtop road running south. It will take you to Alton.

Campbellsburg
Washington County

John I. Morrison of Salem, Indiana was commissioned to lay out a new town along the proposed route of the New Albany and Salem Railroad in western Washington County in August of 1849. The new village was named Buena Vista.

During the next two years Robert Campbell platted an addition to the town. The new subdivision was called Campbellsburg in honor of him. In later years the two communities united under the name of Campbellsburg. The town was incorporated in 1875.

Over the next quarter of a century Campbellsburg became the center of business in western Washington County. The former prosperity of the town is evidenced by the still standing stately homes that grace its tree lined thoroughfares. Some of these stately residences have been restored to their original splendor.

Two events cast dark shadows on Campbellsburg's future. The first devastating blow to Campbellsburg came in the summer of 1904. A fire broke out in the Pollard Livery Barn which destroyed an entire section of the downtown area. Having no fire department the citizenry of Campbellsburg fought the blaze with hapless results. Consumed in the inferno were the Odd Fellow's Hall, Modern Woodsmen's Hall, four business buildings, and several barns and residences.

The second blow to Campbellsburg was the advent of the automobile. Many of the town's residents started driving to Salem, the county seat, which is only eight miles southeast of the community, for business and shopping. This was an economic disaster for Campbellsburg's downtown.

Empty store fronts line Campbellsburg's main street.

By the late 1960's Campbellsburg's business district was lined with abandoned buildings. It has been said that a crisis is the innovator of ideas. The idea of making the unoccupied and historical buildings into a tourist attraction spread through the community. Campbellsburg, at last, had a plan to deal with its deteriorating downtown area.

In 1968 Campbellsburg held its first arts and crafts festival. A block long line of older buildings in the downtown section were turned into craft and art shops. Some of the attractions of the festival were a parade, bicycle races, flea markets, a greased pig contest, and ice cream socials. The old high school gymnasium became the center for the performing arts. Among the attractions were plays, music shows, and hymn sings.

The town still needed a permanent enticement to bring in tourists on a year around basis. To remedy this situation, a unique restaurant, named the Strawberry Barn was started in the remodeled Hardin-Wade general store building. Local people came to the aid of the restaurant by loaning the eating establishment their priceless antiques. The nineteenth century decor and the delicious food contributed to the Strawberry Barn's popularity.

Dining guests from as far away as Louisville, Kentucky and Indianapolis, Indiana came to frequent the restaurant. It seemed that Campbellsburg was on its way up to becoming a living, working town.

Sadly, Campbellsburg's new found prominence was short lived. The Sunday afternoon of April 30, 1972 was no different from any other busy week-end for the restaurant. Patrons crowded through the doors of the Strawberry Barn to enjoy a leisurely afternoon meal. Suddenly, a fire broke out on the second floor of the restaurant. Guests and restaurant help through good sense and cooperation were safely evacuated from the building. Fire companies from Campbellsburg, Mitchell, Salem, and other communities responded to the alarm. As brave as their efforts were, the flames burned the restaurant to the ground. The inferno left the standing concrete walls of the kitchen as mementos of the eating establishment. It was never rebuilt.

After the fire Campbellsburg's business district was again on a downhill slide. The annual celebration named in later years the Strawberry Festival ceased to draw the throngs of people that were necessary to make it a success. Many of the craft shops and related businesses closed their doors leaving the empty store fronts that now line both sides of the main street.

"Never say die" is the last word heard from Campbellsburg. Two antique shops and one hobby shop are still flourishing. Voices are again being heard about revitalizing the downtown shopping area. Time holds the answer for Campbellsburg.

The town is located on Indiana Route 60, fourteen miles southeast of Mitchell, Indiana.

Corydon
Harrison County

Corydon has the distinction of being the Indiana Territory's last capital and the first state capital of Indiana. While Governor of the Indiana Territory William Henry Harrison privately purchased several parcels of land. In 1808 the newly organized Harrison County included some of Harrison's land purchases within its boundries. Governor Harrison named the county seat Corydon from a song that he remembered in the Missouri Harmony songbook.

When the War of 1812 broke out there was political pressure brought to bear in the territorial legislature to move the capital eastward. Some of the legislators feared that the Indians might attack Vincennes. In 1813 by the consent of the legislature the territorial capital was moved from Vincennes to Corydon.

The new seat of government of the Indiana Territory was housed in the then recently built blue limestone Harrison County Courthouse from 1813 to 1816. In 1815, a census revealed that the territory that now comprises Indiana, had the necessary 60,000 population required for statehood. The territorial legislature called a constitutional convention to draw up a plan for the government of the State of Indiana. Between June 10 and 29, 1816 forty three delegates met in Corydon for this purpose. Some of these meetings took place in the courthouse while others took place under a large Elm tree that was later named the Constitutional Elm.

Indiana's first state capital building.

Indiana's first session of its General Assembly took place on November 4, 1816. The Senate and Supreme Court occupied the upstairs of the courthouse while the House of Representatives met on the lower level of the structure. Jonathan Jennings became Indiana's first elected governor.

In 1825 the state capital was moved to Indianapolis. The move was made to accomodate the shifting population patterns in the state.

Corydon's history did not end with the moving of the state capital. On July 9, 1863 Confederate General John Hunt Morgan with approximately 2,500 calvarymen attacked the town. Opposing Morgan were 450 Home guards and citizens under the command of Colonel Lewis Jordon. The skirmish, which is now called the Battle of Corydon, was fought about a mile south of the village. Morgan's raiders overwhelmed the defenders in 25 minutes. They immediately rode into Corydon, looted it, and rode out heading east that same afternoon.

Reportedly, the Home guard suffered four killed and two wounded. One hundred and fifty of the defenders managed to escape while 300 of them were paroled by the victorious Confederate troops. Morgan's losses were estimated to be 10 killed and 40 wounded.

The Corydon State Capital Memorial embraces the old capitol building, the Constitutional Elm, and the home of Indiana's second governor, William Hendricks. Restoration of the capitol building started in 1929. On display in the structure are the memorabilia, antiques, and furnishings from that memorable period.

The Constitutional Elm's trunk has been preserved for posterity by surrounding it with a monument of sandstone.

Governor Hendrick's home, which is a two story brick house, served as his executive headquarters and private residence from 1821 to 1825. In 1975 the State of Indiana bought and restored the governor's mansion.

You can obtain more information by writing to the Corydon State Capital Memorial, 200 North Capitol Avenue, Corydon, Indiana 47112.

There is a brochure that can be obtained at the old capitol building that outlines a walking tour of Corydon. Some of the sights to be seen are the first state office building, the Posey House, the Kinter House, and the Harrison County Fairgrounds. The Harrison County Fair is claimed to be the oldest continuous fair in Indiana. It dates back to 1859.

The old state capitol building is located on Market Street between Beaver and Walnut Street. To reach Corydon take Interstate Route 64 west out of New Albany until you reach the Corydon turn off which will be Indiana Route 135. Turn south on route 135 until it intersects with Indiana Route 337. Turn southeast on route 337 to Corydon.

Hindostan
Martin County

In 1819 a group of investors led by Frederick F. Sholts pooled their resources and laid out a town on the east fork of the White River five and one half miles south of Shoals, Indiana, the present county seat of Martin County. The new settlement was located where there is a seven foot high waterfall in the course of the river. Captain Caleb Fellows, the oldest of the business partners was given the honor of naming the new community. He called it Hindostan. Supposedly Captain Fellows derived the name from his knowledge of India.

Sholts and his colleagues entertained ideas of making Hindostan the rival of Louisville, Kentucky. One of their first moves was to try to make Hindostan the county seat of a new county which they wanted carved out of Daviess and Dubois Counties. Their efforts were successful in this project. The new Martin County was organized in 1820. Being the only town in the new county, Hindostan was named the county seat.

Hindostan enjoyed immediate success as a town. By the end of 1820, it was estimated that over 200 families settled in and around the village. In 1825 the town had two taverns, two stores, a blacksmith shop, a cabinet maker, a wagon maker, a saddler, a millwright, two tailors, two shoe makers, and one carpenter.

Sandstone, quarried in the hills of Orange County, was being hauled by horse drawn wagons and oxcart to a water finishing mill in Hindostan. Here the finished stone, along with other produce, was being shipped by flatboat to New Orleans and other markets. The stone was eventually shaped into many different types of sharpening stones, commonly known as whetstones.

The Hindostan Methodist Church stands on
the crest of a hill just before you reach the turn
off for the old town by that name.

In 1826 one member of the settlement took sick and suddenly died. The unknown disease spread through the community. Within a few months approximately half of the town's 1,200 people perished from what was called the "Great Sickness." When a person contacted the disease he suffered from an uncontrollable temperature. The plague that struck Hindostan is, to this day, a debatable topic.

Survivors of the sickness moved away from Hindostan to a site approximately two and one half miles north up the river which they called Mount Pleasant. The seat of justice of the county moved with the fleeing citizenry.

There is a treasure story associated with the flight from Hindostan. According to the tale the county treasurer buried the county's gold before fleeing the town. When this task was completed he fell victim to the plague and died before he could reveal the location of the burial site.

The Hindostan Falls Fishing Area now occupies the site of the old town. Camping, fishing, boat launching, and picnicking are permitted. During periods of low water part of the rocky river bottom is exposed. People walk out on this stoney peninsula to fish.

Hindostan Falls can be reached by taking Indiana Route 550 southeast out of Loogootee, Indiana. Approximately six miles down the twisting, turning highway you will see on the right side a church and a sign reading Hindostan Methodist Church. Just beyond the church there is a county historical marker giving details of the Hindostan site. A road junctions with Route 550 at the historical plaque. Turn right on this side road. A one half mile drive will bring you to the site of the old town.

Madison
Jefferson County

Madison is the county seat of Jefferson County. It is situated on the Ohio River approximately 50 miles from Louisville, Kentucky and approximately 75 miles from Cincinnati, Ohio. At one time Madison rivaled these cities in the commercial and cultural leadership of the Ohio River Valley.

The first known white man's cabin in present day Madison was constructed in 1808. Messrs. John Paul, Lewis Davis, and Jonathan Lyon laid out the town in 1810. The following year lots were being sold to the public. In 1816 Madison had three or four brick homes, about 20 frame ones, and probably over 100 log cabins. Madison was incorporated as a town on April 15, 1824, and as a city by act of the legislature in 1838.

Madison became the gateway to the settlement of the Northwest Territory when the first railroad constructed west of the Alleghenies ran

The James F. D. Lanier State Memorial.

from the town to Indianapolis. People of all backgrounds and occupations migrated to Madison. In 1834 the population of Madison was estimated at 2,500 in 1840 it was estimated at 3,798, and in 1850 it was estimated at over 7,000. For a while Madison was the largest city in Indiana.

Madison, because of being a river port and terminus of a railroad was ideally suited for industry. Some of the early manufacturers were the Lewis and Crawford's and Farnsworth, and Honore's foundries and machine shops, Greggs' oil mill, Whitney and Hendricks oil mill and woolen factory, King and Ely's cotton factory, Heberhart's candle plant, Lane's lard oil mill, and the Page, White, and Griffin's steam flouring mills.

Modern day Madison is a city proud of its past and confident of its future. In 1973 our Madison's downtown area had the distinction of being placed on the National Register of Historic Places. The designated area encompasses over 130 city blocks.

One of the main points of interest in Madison is the James F. D. Lanier State Memorial located at 511 West First Street. Lanier moved to Madison when he was just seventeen years old. His personal drive vaulted him into a banking and political career which made him Madison's most influential promoter. Lanier was the chief sponsor of Indiana's first state highway and railroad: the Michigan Road and the Madison and Indianapolis Railroad. He came to Indiana's aid in 1863 when he made an unsecured loan to the state to pay the Indiana soldiers fighting in the Civil War. The state legislature refused to pass an appropriation bill to meet this payroll.

The James F. D. Lanier mansion was designed by noted architect Francis Costigan. Construction was completed in 1844. The southern styled mansion has a huge front yard that nearly runs down to the Ohio

River Bank. Visitors to the Memorial will see many of the Lanier's original furnishings. Sadly, Mrs. Lanier passed on just four years after the couple moved into their new home. James F. D. Lanier moved to New York City after his wife's death where he successfully continued his investment career. The state memorial is open all year from 9 to 12 and from 1 to 4:30. An admission is charged.

There are a number of other homes and buildings open to the public. Among these are the Shrewsbury House, Judge Jeremiah Sullivan's house, Dr. William Hutchings' office and hospital, the Jefferson County Historical Museum, and the Jefferson County Court House. Antique and specialty shops abound in the community. Write or stop at the Tourist Center located at 201 Vaughn Drive, 47250 in Madison for further information.

In 1886 Madison erected a tiered water fountain called the "Centennial Fountain," just north of Main Street on Broadway. The original idea of erecting the fountain was to provide visitors with a place to drink water without imposing on the citizens of the town.

Over the decades the fountain, surrounding sidewalks, and landscaping suffered from deterioration and neglect. The present mayor, Dr. Warren R. Rucker, impaneled a committee to study the problems of renovating the fountain. Eleftherios Karkadoulias, noted for his restoration projects, was given the job of restoring the historical site.

Karkadoulias worked three years on the project. On August 9 of this year, water once again spewed forth from Madison's Centennial Fountain.

Clifty Falls State Park is located just to the west of Madison. The park, covering over 1,360 acres has a motor lodge, two swimming pools, an enlarged camping ground, and an extensive system of walking trails to view the falls and cataracts of Clifty Creek.

Visit the campus of Hanover College located a few miles to the west of the state park. It was founded in 1827. The magnificient red brick buildings on the college grounds are a sight to behold. Linger awhile at the campus overlook of the Ohio River. The view from this point is inspiring.

Madison is served by Indiana Routes 7 and 62, and U. S. Route 421.

Newburgh
Warrick County

Newburgh, just a few miles to the east of Evansville, Indiana, was one of the first settlements in Warrick County. John Sprinkle, who is claimed to be the first white settler in the county, laid out a town of 105 lots in 1818. In honor of its founder the town was named Sprinkleburg. Over the ensuing years the town became known as Mt. Prospect. Around 1830 a new housing addition was constructed which was called Newburgh. In 1837 the state legislature united these two housing developments under the name of Newburgh.

For years Newburgh was the commercial outlet for Warrick County. The town, being situated on the high bank of the Ohio River far above the high water line, offered excellent docking facilities for the largest boats on the river. By 1885 Newburgh was past its zenith as a busy river port.

Newburgh was captured by the Confederate forces during the Civil War. On July 18, 1862, Brigadier General Adam R. Johnson led a band of guerrilla forces across the Ohio River to confiscate supplies and ammunition. The town was taken without the rattle of musketry.

Modern day Newburgh reflects its past. The street that runs parellel with the river just above the water line is crowded with abandoned and burned out business buildings. Looking down this thoroughfare it is not hard to imagine that it was once a thriving business street.

Higher up the side of the bluff Indiana Route 662 runs parallel with the river. Many stately and well preserved brick and frame homes line this roadway. Here you will find numerous historical plaques attached to the buildings or hanging on posts giving the history of the structure.

Abandoned and burned out buildings
line the street along the
Ohio River in Newburgh.

Indiana Route 662 east out of Evansville will take you to Newburgh. Worthy of visiting and just a few miles to the west of Newburgh, in Evansville, is the Angel Mounds State Memorial. The Indian mounds took its name from the former owner of the property. A flourishing prehistoric native

American town once existed on this site between 1300-1500 A.D. The ancient town and mounds were constructed by a people belonging to a cultural complex called Mississippian. Many of the ancient mud and grass plastered dwellings have been reconstructed on their original locations. An interpretive center houses a simulated archaeological excavation and other exhibits explaining the culture of the town's occupants.

Angel Mounds State Memorial is located at 8216 Pollack Avenue, Evansville, Indiana 47715. The memorial is open daily from 9 to 5. It is closed on Sunday morning from November through March and all other legal holidays except Memorial Day, Independence Day, and Labor Day. There is an admission charge.

New Harmony
Posey County

New Harmony was founded in 1814 by a group called the Harmony Society. They were Lutheran dissenters from Wurtemburg, Germany, who had previously established a colony in Pennsylvania before moving to Indiana.

The Harmonists were led by George Rapp and his adopted son Frederick. They believed that the second coming of Christ would happen in their lifetimes and therefore should subjugate their personal desires for the good of the community. The principle aim of the group was to raise enough money to transport the society to Jerusalem to receive the Lord.

Members of the society practiced celibacy to eliminate the cost of raising children. Single members of the group lived in dormitories, while members that were married prior to joining the society lived platonically in separate households with their families.

Thomas Dean, a native of the State of New York, traveled to Indiana in 1817. He made the following entry in his personal journal about his group's stay at the Harmonist colony on July 13, 1817.

"In the morning we prepared for meeting and went to their forenoon meeting. They had a very good meeting house and there were three or four hundred of the Harmonists assembled. They were the whole, with the exception of ourselves and two or three others. The minister, by the name of Rapp; delivered a discourse in the German tongue which we could not understand; they sang in the same language, and appeared very solemn and severe in their devotions. After the meeting (half past 10 A.M.) we went to look at their fields, vineyards, etc."

The industriousness and self denial of the Harmonists produced results that amazed the critics. In 10 years time they had built four multi-storied brick dormitories; a huge brick church; a large fort-granary; and 126 brick, frame, and log homes. There were 2,000 acres under cultivation with large vineyards and orchards stretching out over the countryside. A portable greenhouse was used to raise oranges and lemons.

The members of the society that did not work on the farms were employed in the town's industries. New Harmony had two distilleries; a brewery; cotton, hemp, woolen, and saw mills; a mechanic's shop; tanyard; and shoe shop.

Rapp decided to move his community back to Pennsylvania in 1825 because of the great distances to market and the feeling that hard work was the prerequisite for keeping the members of the society occupied with its goals.

Robert Owen, a Welsh industrialist and William Maclure, a Scottish philanthropist, purchased New Harmony for $190,000 in the above mentioned year. They believed that a new and better life could be obtained through education. Because of their influence, leading scientists and educators from Europe and the United States settled in New Harmony. Almost from the start the members of the new community started quarreling about the difficulty and the importance of each other's work. Owen's and Maclure's "empire of good sense" failed in 1827. Their good sense seemed to falter when it forgot to include the practical business men and farmers to produce the basic needs of the community.

Many of the scientists and educators remained in New Harmony. Over the years the settlement contributed many firsts to our present day society. Among these were the first kindergarten, the first infant school, the first trade school, the first free public school, the first free library, the first civic dramatic club, and the first seat of the U. S. Geological Survey.

The New Harmony State Memorial preserves five historically significant structures and sites that can be visited by the public. They are the Fauntleroy Home, Dormitory Number 2, the Opera House, the Labyrinth, and the Harmonist Cemetery.

Visitors to the Harmonist Cemetery will be amazed by the lack of tombstones in the burial plot. The Harmonists believed in burying their dead in unmarked graves because this made the interred as equal in death as they were in life. There are over 200 members of the society buried in the cemetery. Prior to the arrival of the white man the Indians constructed burial mounds on this plot.

The Fauntleroy Home was constructed in 1814 by the Harmonists. Several outstanding statesmen, scientists, and educators occupied the home. When Robert Fauntleroy purchased the residence in 1840 his name became permanently associated with the structure. The home is furnished with items dating back to New Harmony's days of glory.

Dormitory Number Two was one of the four large brick buildings constructed by the Harmonists. It housed some of the unmarried male members of the society. Today, the dormitory serves as a display center featuring a collection of artifacts from the Harmonist, Owen, and later periods.

The Opera House was the last communal dormitory built by the Harmonists. Members of the Owen community used it as a ballroom. In 1888 the building was enlarged to provide more space for theatrical activities. At one time it was the second largest theatre in Indiana. The opera house is still being used for the performing arts.

The small stone temple in
the middle of the labyrinth.

Another unusual site at the Memorial is the Labyrinth. This is an intricate maze of shrubbery bordered paths leading to a small temple in the center of it. Symbolically, the winding paths represent the difficulty of achieving harmony. The rough exterior of the temple indicates that harmony offers few allurements to those that do not possess it, while the beautiful interior of the temple symbolizes the rewards of attaining harmony.

The original labyrinth fell in disrepair several years after the Harmonists left for Pennsylvania. In 1939 the State of Indiana rebuilt the garden maze adjacent to the original site.

Presently, many of the other original Harmonist buildings are being restored. Some of these will be open to the public in forthcoming years.

In October of 1979 the new visitor center called the Atheneum opened up at New Harmony. The building contains four exhibition galleries for permanent and changing exhibits, a theatre, observation terraces on several levels, and a visitor orientation area where there is centralized computer ticketing for the Historic New Harmony Tour.

The Atheneum commands a sweeping view of the Wabash River and the northwest corner of the town. It is open seven days a week, year-round, 9 to 5. For more information write to the Visitor Center, Historic New Harmony, New Harmony, Indiana 47631.

While in New Harmony drive out to the 3,272 acre Harmonie State Recreation Area. It is located four miles south of the town. There are facilities for camping, fishing, hiking, swimming, and picnicking.

Indiana Route 66 west out of Evansville will take you to New Harmony.

Pigeon Roost
Scott County

In 1809 a group of settlers led by William Collins established a small community near the southern boundary of present day Scott County. The settlement took its name from Pigeon Creek that flowed through the area. Thousands of passenger pigeons roosted along the banks of the stream.

Initially, the Indians in the vicinity paid little heed to the pioneers as they hacked farms out of the woodlands, built roads, and laid out new towns. The settlers would occasionally see the Indians filing along the game trails in search of prey. Conniving British agents united with Tecumseh and the Prophet to incite the Indians against the continual migration of new settlers to the Indiana Territory. Stopping this influx of new arrivals was in reality, preserving the Indian way of life.

When the War of 1812 broke out, some of the men from Pigeon Roost went off to join General William Henry Harrison's North-western army. This drain of manpower left the small community ill prepared to cope with a possible Indian attack. Seemingly, the men that volunteered for Harrison's forces gave this little thought.

In the early evening of September 5, 1812, a band of approximately 10 to 12 Indians, believed to be mostly Shawnee, besieged Pigeon Roost. The warriors plundered and burned the cabins. Nine adults and 15 children died during the Indian raid. According to one report a Mrs. Beadle and her two small children concealed themselves in a sinkhole while the braves ravaged the settlement. She, along with her two children, managed to escape on foot six miles to the nearest settlement.

A large force of men was formed at Charleston and vicinity, located to the south in Clark County, to hunt down the raiders. By chance or planning the Indians were able to elude the pursuers by fording the flooding Muscatatuck River.

The victims of the assault were buried in a mass grave at the foot of a giant Sassafras tree. In 1904, a 44 foot monument was erected at the site to commemorate this unfortunate incident.

Today, Pigeon Roost is the simplest and probably the least visited state memorial in Indiana. It consists of the monument and a small picnic ground. Immediately to the west of the memorial is a small cemetery.

Walking among the tombstones my son-in-law Larry and I noticed the name of Collins on a number of them. My mind flashed back to the circumstances of this tragedy. thought to myself, "Two opposing cultures clashed here to preserve their way of life. If honest, reasonable, and cooler heads would have prevailed in those days, then, maybe, this page of history would have never been written. Then, maybe, we would still have Indian owned land in Indiana."

I told Larry, "I'm coming back here someday for a picnic. This place gives me food for thought."

Pigeon Roost State Memorial.

Larry replied, "You're right Harry. In a way, I find it kind of peaceful here."

With that we returned to the car and headed for our next destination.

To reach the Pigeon Roost State Memorial take U. S. Route 31 south out of Scottsburg, Indiana. Approximately six miles down the highway look for the state memorial sign. The site is located on the east side of the road just over the railroad tracks.

Portersville
Dubois County

Portersville was the first county seat of Dubois County. It was probably selected for this distinction because the town straddled the east fork of the White River. Rafts and barges docked at the village to pick up farm produce for shipment down river. It is said Portersville's prosperous years ran from 1818 to 1830.

According to one story an early pioneer by the name of Arthur Harbison called the town Portersville in honor of one of his relatives. However, history also tells us that a Dr. Porter was an early prominent citizen in the community. It seems more likely that the town was named after him.

The county courthouse in Portersville was a two story structure made out of hand hewn logs with brick chimneys at each end of the building. On court days in the warmer months the jury camped at what became known as "Jury Spring," one-quarter of a mile south of the village. Those people with cases waiting to be heard camped around the courthouse.

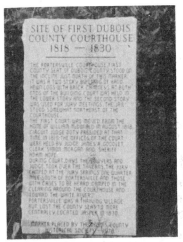

In 1830 the more centrally located town of Jasper became the county seat. This event led to the decline of Portersville.

Today, Portersville is a quaint little rural village. Although few in number, most of the houses are well kept. In 1978 the Dubois County Historical Society placed a stone marker at the approximate site of the old courthouse. The saloons and other businesses that flourished

This historical marker in Portersville gives details about Dubois County's first courthouse.

in the village have long since made their exits into oblivion. I was unable to locate a tavern or eating establishment in the town.

An abandoned coal strip mine is located just to the south of the community. The poor quality of the coal forced its closure.

Portersville can be reached by taking U. S. Route 231 north out of Jasper, Indiana. Continue north until you make a junction with the Portersville Road. An old metal sign and sign post marks this spot. Turn west and follow the county road in that direction. Make a right turn on the first county road running north. An eight mile ride on this country thoroughfare will take you to Portersville.

Spring Mill Village
Franklin County

In 1814 Samuel Jackson Jr., a young Canadian, and his family settled in a valley near the mouth of what is known today as Hamer Cave. Utilizing water power from the nearby cavern, Jackson built a mill out of logs.

The wealthy Bullitt brothers from Louisville, Kentucky purchased Jackson's property in 1817. They constructed a three story grist mill made of limestone that was quarried in the surrounding hills. Today this building makes up part of the pioneer village located in Spring Mill State Park.

In 1823 the Bullitt brothers sold the mill, at a substantial profit, to another set of brothers, the Montgomerys of Philadelphia, Pennsylvania. The new owners added a water powered sawmill to the existing facilities.

The grist mill at Spring Mill Village.

This was followed by the building of a tavern and distillery. A post office under the name of Arcole Village was established at the site in 1828.

The Montgomerys, due to illness, sold the village in 1832 to two other enterprising brothers, the Hamers. Under their direction the village reached its peak of prosperity in the middle 1800's. Hugh Hamer, the miller, changed the name of the village to Spring Mill.

It is said in its heyday, the grist mill operated day and night during harvest time. During this period, according to the story, farmers had to wait nine or ten days in line to get their corn or wheat ground into meal.

The village had a general store, hat shop, leather shop, and a country doctor that worked out of his apothecary shop. Some people, at that time, believed that Spring Mill Village was going to become the commercial center of that part of Franklin County.

Sadly, the village's grasp for future prosperity was stymied by two events that they counld not control. First the development of the internal combustion engine made water power obsolete. Secondly, the railroad that was supposed to service the town refused to lay its tracks into the valley. Jonathan Turley, the last owner of the mill, closed down the entire operation in 1892.

Through the efforts of the local populace the village and surrounding area was made into a state park in 1927. Restoration of the old settlement was started that year.

Spring Mill State Park offers visitors a multitude of activities for their enjoyment. There are facilities for boating, camping, cave trips, fishing, hiking, picnicking, horseback riding, and swimming. The park has an inn that is open all year.

Work is still going on to improve the buildings and displays at the village. The grist mill, which is in daily operation from April through October, sells cornmeal to the tourists. Visitors strolling through the old settlement will find an apothecary shop, village store, shoemakers, tavern, distillery, hatmakers shop, weaver's, meeting house, and several log houses.

The Hamer Cemetery, which is uphill from the village, was first used in 1832. Many residents of the village are interred there.

A person can leave the pioneer period and enter the space age at the park. The Virgil I. Grissom Memorial is located in its confines. Grissom, a native of Mitchell, was one of the seven original astronauts and the second man to travel in space. On display at the memorial are his space suit, the "Molly Brown" Gemini space capsule, and a montage of pictures.

Spring Mill State Park is located on Indiana Route 60 just a few miles east of the town of Mitchell. For further information write to Spring Mill State Park, Box 376, Mitchell, Indiana 47446.

Vincennes
Knox County

Vincennes, which is the oldest city in Indiana, traces its origin back to 1702, when a Catholic parish was claimed to have been established in the area of the present town.

In 1734 Morgane Le Seur de Vincene was given orders by the French governor to establish a line of fortifications to protect the lucrative fur trade from encroachment by the British. The French fur traders in Vincennes followed the life style of Indians, by living in crude huts and cabins. When Le Seur de Vincene arrived in the settlement he brought with him traders, craftsmen, farmers, boatsmen, and soldiers. The new arrivals called the village "Aux Poste."

Le Seur de Vincene was killed by the Chickasaw Indians on the lower Mississippi River while establishing the above mentioned fortifications. St. Ange replaced Vincene as post commandant at the French outpost on the Wabash River. The inhabitants of the community continued to call their town Vincennes out of respect for their fallen leader.

St. Ange started Vincennes on the way to becoming a developed community. He served as post commander until the land was ceded to the British upon the conclusion of the French and Indian War (1754-1763).

George Rogers Clark carried the American Revolution to the old Northwest when he and his men attacked and seized the British fort at Kaskaskia (Illinois) on July 4, 1778. Clark, knowing that his campaign would not be a success without taking Fort Sackville (Vincennes) prepared to attack it. On February 9, 1779, Clark with 127 men started the incredible march across 180 miles of (drowned country) flooded land to Fort Sackville. His army reached the English garrison on February 23. The British commander, Colonel Henry Hamilton, surrendered his forces to Clark's army on February 25, 1779. This capitulation threw open the door to American settlement of the old Northwest.

In 1800, Congress established the Indiana Territory. William Henry Harrison was appointed its first governor that same year. Harrison's authority extended over the present states of Indiana, Illinois, Wisconsin, Michigan, and part of Minnesota. Vincennes was named the capital of the territory.

France, in 1803, sold all its territory west of the Mississippi River to the United States. The Louisiana Purchase, as it came to be known, was governed from Vincennes for the first year.

William Henry Harrison remained governor of the Indiana Territory until September 12, 1812. He resigned to become Commander-in-Chief of the army of the Northwest in the War of 1812.

Vincennes, today, is a showboat of history. Some of the many sights to be seen are the George Rogers Clark Memorial National Historical Park, the Indiana Territory State Memorial, the William Henry Harrison Mansion "Grouseland," the Old State Bank State Memorial, and Vincennes University, (founded in 1801.)

While on the campus of Vincennes University stop at the Log Cabin Tourist Center. Here you can catch the open air bus called the Trailblazer. The bus will take you along the old town's "Mile of History." It is a stimulating ride. For more information about the sights of Vincennes write to the Log Cabin Tourist Center, First and Harrison Street, Vincennes, Indiana 47591.

The famed, Gimbels Department Store chain, with its outlets from New York City to Milwaukee, Wisconsin started in Vincennes. One wonders when Ed Gimbel and his seven sons opened their first store at Second and Waters Streets in town whether they envisioned such a department store domain.

When in Vincennes it is possible to step out of the historical period and into the prehistoric age. The Sonotabac Prehistoric Indian Mound and Museum located at 2401 Wabash Avenue afford you this opportunity. In the museum you can browse at your own leisure viewing the various exhibits and artifacts that take a person back to 8,000 B.C.

The Sonotabac Prehistoric Indian Mound.

The mound is named in honor of the son of Tabac, a patriotic Indian chief, who befriended George Rogers Clark in his capture of Fort Sackville. It is the largest prehistoric Indian mound in Indiana.

People of the Hopewell culture constructed the mound around 300 B.C. Evidence indicates the mound was built for religious purposes. Visitors can climb the wooden stairs leading up the side of the elevation to its summit.

There is a small admission charge to visit the museum and Indian mound.

The Blessings Of Your Indiana Heritage

This lecture was given by the author at the Unity Church in Hammond, Indiana on Sunday, August 19, 1979 at 11:00 A.M.

"It all started as one of my colleagues, Chuck Pearson, and I sat in Doc Rosecrans' one room cabin nestled on the desert to the west of the Superstition Mountains in Arizona. Doc has a lot of visitors dropping by to see him because of the book he wrote on the Dutchman Mine and numerous hunts for this fabled bonanza.

One of Doc's friends named Steve was there that night. Our conversation, as usual, centered on the Dutchman mine. Steve, who originally was from the Midwest, stated, "Harry you're a good writer, why don't you write something on the prehistoric mound builders in the East. We have plenty of Indian ruins out here, but I believe, if I'm not mistaken, the mound builders predate them."

With this impetus, our conversation turned to the mound builders of Indiana and Illinois. It was then I found out how little I knew about the history of my own area. When Chuck and I left Doc's that night the idea was implanted in my mind to write something about Indiana and the surrounding states.

I, as most of us do, got carried up in other activities such as the prehistoric copper mining Indians of Michigan's upper peninsula and the Lost Adams Gold Diggings in New Mexico. While doing research on these subjects I was completing the first drafts of two additional books on the Lost Dutchman Mine. One is a children's book and the other is a biographical account of my experiences hunting the ever elusive gold bonanza.

I approached my good friend and sometimes very critical editor George Warnecke about doing something on the Hoosier state. We discussed the idea at length, but somehow I managed to put it out of my mind for the time being. You might say, I was a bit lazy.

Last winter I gave a slide show here at the church on the prehistoric Indians of the Southwest. Many of you people were kind enough to remain after the service for a potluck dinner and my presentation. Upon the conclusion of my program several kind people asked me why I didn't do a book on Indiana. If you recall, I stated that I planned to. From then on every once in a while someone here at the church would ask me, "How's the Indiana book coming?"

My wife Marilyn and I got caught up with an idea for the Indiana book, hence my recent research on our state.

I would like to start our overview of Indiana's history with the mound builders.

Let's go back 2,000 years for a moment to see what was taking place at the Sonotabac Indian Mound located at present day Vincennes.

In the early morning we see the religious leader of the Indian settlement step out of his hut which is built on the top of the mound. The ancient clergyman faces east toward the rising sun. He then performs some mystic rites which are unknown to us today.

The Hopewell Indian villagers called their religious leader, "The Brother Of The Sun." They worshipped a heavenly father who dwelled in the earth and the sky. The only visible giver of growth, warmth and light was the sun; to them it was God's eye.

Indiana was covered with mounds from these ancient cultures. Most of them were built between 500 B.C. and 500 A.D. They were constructed for religious purposes, burial purposes, and in some cases a combination of both of them. On some occasions they constructed effigy mounds. A nearby example of this is the Great Serpent Mound in Ohio. This mound wiggles across the countryside like a crawling snake. You have to be above the mound to see the shape of the serpent. Did ancient astronauts guide their space vehicles on these odd shaped mounds? Most archaeologists think not.

Two of the best examples of the mound builders handwork in Indiana are located at the Mounds State Park in Anderson, Indiana and at the Angel Mounds State Memorial in Evansville, Indiana. It is estimated that over 2,000 people lived at the Angel Mound site.

The prehistoric Indians for reasons that are not fully known today disappeared from their villages. The transition from the prehistoric Indians to the historic Indians again is not fully understood. It is believed that various bands of Miami and Potawatomi Indians occupied the state from time to time. The Potawatomi and Miami moved in mass to Indiana in the seventeenth century. They came from the present day states of Wisconsin and Illinois. Other Indian residents of the state were Shawnee, Munsee, Mohegan, Kickapoo, Delaware, Wea, and the Piankeshaw. It is not hard to see why Indiana was named after the Indians.

There is a dispute among the scholars of who was the first white man to enter what is now Indiana. Some believe that Father Marquette on his way back to Fort St. Joseph, which was located near the present city of Niles Michigan, stopped at the mouth of the Grand Calumet River in what is now Gary, Indiana, in April of 1675.

The first authentic written account of the white man entering Indiana tells us about Robert LaSalle's party portaging from the St. Joseph River to the Kankakee River on December 5, 1679. A marker commemorating this historic site stands in the present day Riverview Cemetery in South Bend, Indiana.

Between 1700 and 1763 Indiana was part of the French Colonial Empire. The French were primarily interested in fur trading. They mingled well with the Indians and in many cases married them. During this period the French built military stockades, although there may be some disputes or the dates, at Quiatenon (near Lafayette) in 1717, at Fort Miami (Fort Wayne) in 1721, and Vincennes in 1734. What we see here is that the history of the white man in what is now Indiana started in the north and moved south. It is generally thought the oldest part of the state, referring to the white man's habitation, started in the south and moved north. As we can see, it is just the opposite.

Because of the British victory in the French and Indian War, Indiana was under British control from 1763 to 1783. They tried to keep the American colonists east of the Appalachian Mountains. History records the British continuing the fur trade with the Indians, but the feeling of equality the red man experienced with the French was gone. In some instances the British considered the Indians as primitives.

The American Revolution started in 1775 and lasted to 1783. Most of the fighting took place in the Eastern states, but Indiana was also involved in that conflict. At the beginning of the war the British dominated Ohio, Indiana, Illinois, Michigan, and Wisconsin from their fort formerly located at present day Detroit, Michigan. The British incited the Indians to attack the American settlers in Kentucky, which was then claimed by the State of Virginia. Governor Patrick Henry of Virginia commissioned George Rogers Clark a lieutenant colonel in the Virginia militia. He was given an authorization to raise 350 men and spend $6,000 for supplies and ammunition. Clark was given secret orders to take Kaskaskia, Illinois and possibly Detroit. On July 4, 1778 Kaskaskia fell to Clark and 170 men without a shot being fired. The British Lieutenant-governor at Detroit, Colonel Henry Hamilton, marched to Fort Sackville (Vincennes) and took it from an American force comprised of Captain Helm and two regulars on December 17, 1778. Colonel Hamilton planned to attack Clark at Kaskaskia the following spring.

Colonel Clark with 127 men struck out for Fort Sackville. The American expedition had to cross 180 miles of flooded land (drowned country). Clark's forces arrived at Fort Sackville on February 23, 1779. The seige at the fort lasted until February 25, 1779. On that date Colonel Hamilton formally surrendered. Because of this victory the Northwest Territory was thrown open for American settlement.

The George Rogers Clark National Memorial in Vincennes now stands on the site of Fort Sackville.

One of the greatest Indians that lived in the Hoosier state, and for that matter, the nation, was Little Turtle, Chief of the Miamis. His first victory over a white man's army was in November of 1780. A French solider of fortune named LaBalme led a small army of Creoles from Vincennes to attack the British garrison at Detroit. On his way north LaBalme stopped long enough to destroy an Indian village at Fort Wayne. On November 5,

780, the Indians under the leadership of Little Turtle attacked and destroyed the Creole Army. In October of 1790 Little Turtle's forces defeated an American militia force commanded by Colonel John Hardin.

Little Turtle's greatest victory came in November of 1791 when he defeated General Arthur St. Clair's expeditionary forces sent to clear northern Ohio of the Indians. The battle known as St. Clair's Massacre was fought approximately ten miles east of Portland, Indiana in Ohio. One third of St. Clair's 2,700 man army was lost. This was the greatest defeat an American army suffered up till that time.

The Miami chief, realizing that further resistance against the Americans was fruitless, turned his back on the ways of war for the ways of peace. He visited Presidents George Washington, John Adams, and Thomas Jefferson. Little Turtle was instrumental in establishing an agricultural school to teach the Indians the white man's ways of farming.

Jacob Piatt Dunn, the famous Indiana historian has paid the following tribute to the great chief, "He was the greatest of the Miamis, and perhaps, by the standard of achievement, which is the fairest of all standards, the greatest Indian the world has known. All Hoosiers should be proud of this Indian chief, and he deserves to be remembered with the greatest historical figures in the history of our state."

And I say to you, how many of us have ever heard of him.

Congress by the Ordinance of 1787 established the Northwest Territory. In 1800 Congress divided this territory into two separate areas. The Indiana Territory included the present states of Indiana, Illinois, Wisconsin, Michigan, and part of Minnesota. On May 13, 1800 William Henry Harrison became Governor of the Indiana Territory. Harrison later, with the title of general, led an American army against the Indian confederacy engineered by the Shawnee brothers, Tecumseh and the Prophet. At 4:00 A.M. on November 7, 1811 the Prophet led his men in an attack on Harrison's army near the confluence of the Tippecanoe and Wabash Rivers. The Prophet's army was sent in flight after a two hour engagement. This clash became known as the Battle of Tippecanoe.

The Tippecanoe Battle Ground is now a state memorial. It is located on Ninth Street Road south of the town of Battleground, Indiana.

Harrison was elected ninth president of the United States. He died in office, 31 days after his inauguration, on April 4, 1841.

The territorial capital moved from Vincennes to Corydon, Indiana in 1813. Corydon became the first state capital when Indiana became the 19th state admitted to the Union on December 11, 1816.

Organized Indian resistance against the Americans came to a halt at the close of the War of 1812 in 1815. Because of this there was a great migration of southern farmers into our state.

One of the black marks on Indiana's record was the forced removal of a Potawatomi Indian village in 1838. The village leader, Chief Menominee, had not signed the treaty that gave up the Indian lands to the white settlers. He therefore believed that he was not bound by the treaty's terms. The then governor of Indiana, David Wallace, ordered the state militia to help the Indian agent force the Indians off their lands. Chief Menominee's village was located eight miles south of Plymouth, Indiana. The Indians were supposedly given new land in the present State of Kansas. On September 4, 1838, 859 Potawatomi Indians left for the 665 mile journey to the Jayhawk state. They arrived there on November 4, 1838. Over 150 Indians lost their lives or strayed from the main body before they reached their new home. This tragic episode became known as the "Trail of Death."

The little town of New Harmony in Posey County, which is in the extreme Southwest section of Indiana, became the scene of two very important experiments in community living. In 1814 George Rapp and his followers, called Harmonists, founded the town. New Harmony prospered as an agricultural and industrial center. Rapp sold the town in 1825 to Robert Owen, a Welsh industrialist and William Maclure, a Scottish philanthropist. Owen and Maclure, believing that education was the key to a better way of life assembled a group of renowned teachers and scientists from Europe and the Eastern United States to help establish their "empire of good sense." What they forgot to remember was the fact that some intellectuals shy away from physical work. There was too much intellectualism and not enough farming and horse shoeing. The town failed in 1827.

New Harmony contributed many firsts to our present day society. Among them were the first infant school, the first kindergarten, the first trade school, the first free public school system, the first free library, the first civic dramatic club, and the first seat of the U. S. Geological Survey.

Between 1830 and 1860 Indiana was a state on the move. Steam boats replaced the flatboats during this era. The towns along the Ohio River such as Lawrenceburg, Vevay, Aurora, Madison, New Albany, Jeffersonville, Alton, Tell City, Newburgh, Evansville, and Mount Vernon became busy river ports.

Indiana experienced an era of canal building during this same period. Three great canals were planned, the Wabash and Erie, the Central, and the Whitewater. The canals were plagued with frequent flooding and high maintenance costs. With the coming of the railroads the canal age faded into history. Indiana has commemorated the canal era by establishing the Whitewater Canal State Memorial at Metamora, Indiana. Here you can take a horse drawn canal boat down the old waterway.

Levi Coffin, a successful Quaker businessman and bank director became known as the President of the underground railroad during this same period of time. His home served as a haven and rest stop for over 2,000 slaves fleeing the southern United States for their freedom in Canada. Mr. Coffin's home, located in Fountain, Indiana is now a state memorial.

Indiana suffered a tinge of the Civil War on July 8, 1863 when Brigadier General John Hunt Morgan of the Confederate States of America swept through Southern Indiana with 2,500 confederate cavalrymen. Morgan crossed the Ohio River at Mauckport, Indiana. He captured Salem, Indiana and then turned northeast bound for Ohio. Altogether he was in Indiana for five days.

Confederate soldiers being held at the unheated Camp Morton Military Prison in Indianapolis found death from exposure staring them in the face on an extremely cold night in early 1862. True to Hoosier hospitality, private citizens offered to take some the Confederate prisoners, many of them wounded, into their homes. The prison commandant Colonel Richard Owen, released the prisoners on their pledge to return to the prison the next morning. There is no doubt that through the kindness of Colonel Owen and the humanity of the citizens of Indianapolis, many Confederate lives were saved that night. Reportedly, the next morning, all the paroled Confederate soldiers returned to the prison.

Colonel Owen, at a later date, was captured by the Confederates in Kentucky. The Confederates released Colonel Owen out of gratitude for the kindness and fairness that he had extended to their comrades. Some fifty years later, descendents of the involved Confederate soldiers and some actual Confederate veterans pooled their resources to purchase a bust of Colonel Owen, which now can be seen in the main hall of the Indiana State House.

If there is such a thing as greatness, and I believe there is, those people involved in this incident surely had it.

The unsung heroes of Indiana's past and its present day are the people. The people that live in the towns, cities, and in the country. Most of us are familar with the paintings of the old country churches on the hilltop. They can still be seen if you take the time to travel the byways of this nation. Usually you will find a cemetery along side, behind, or across the road from the churches. Whenever I walk through these silent resting places glancing at the dates on the stones, I wonder what stories these individuals from the 1800's could tell us. The story we do know is that today's life style was made possible through their efforts. They are the ones that filled the ranks of the armies, they are the ones that cleared the land and plowed the fields, they are the ones that put their shoulders to the grindstone in the primitive factories of that day. They are the ones that should be immortalized.

The same holds true for our era. Through our efforts we will either bless or curse our descendants. My hope is that when our history is written, they will say of us, God Bless them, they didn't let us down.

After the Civil War Indiana started her climb to becoming the urbanized, industrialized, and agricultural state we know today.

For some strange reason, and I know not why, Hoosier authors started piling up one national best seller after another starting in the 1870's. This golden age of Literature began with Edward Eggleston when he wrote **Th** **Hoosier School Master** in 1871. **Ben Hur** by General Lew Wallac followed in 1880. In 1883 James Whitcomb Riley's **Old Swimming Hol** was published. Before Riley was through, he vied Henry Wadswort Longfellow as America's most popular poet. I still chuckle at Riley's poer titled, **The Passing Of The Backhouse.** Charles Major's **Whe Knighthood Was In Flower** came out in 1898. **Alice Of Old Vincenne** by Maurice Thompson was published in 1900. George Ade's **Fables I Slang** came out that same year. Ade went on to write several successfu musical comedies. Some of these were **The County Chairman, Th College Widow,** and the **Sultan of Sulu.** Theodore Dreiser wrote **Siste Carrie** in 1900 and **An American Tragedy** in 1925. His brother, althougl he spelled his last name different, Paul Dresser, wrote **On The Banks O The Wabash** in 1899. He wrote hit tune after hit tune around this sam period of time. In 1904 Gene Stratton Porter's **Freckles** came out. Thi was the beginning of a long line of best selling novels by her. It is said tha she had a readership of over 50,000,000 people. Booth Tarkington' **Penrod** was published in 1914. He went on to write a series of popula songs and novels. Ernie Pyle made literary fame as a war correspondent ir Word War II. Sadly, he lost his life in that conflict. Jessamyn West' **Friendly Persuasion** came out in 1940. Her great literary efforts have blessed us into the 1970's. Ross F. Lockridge Jr. wrote his great nove **Raintree County** in 1948. **But We Were Born Free** by Elmer Davis came out in 1954. Jean Shepherd's **In God We Trust, All Others Pay Cash** and other best selling novels keeps Indiana represented at the top o today's literary world.

For lack of a better explanation for this parade of great Hoosier authors, I would like to quote Mr. Dale Burgess, himself a Hoosier author, on the subject. He stated simply, "Maybe it's something in the drinking water."

One of Indiana's most famous artists was T. C. Steele. He was instrumental in the founding of the Brown County Art Colony. Steele painted the beauty of that county on canvas. His home, which is located one mile south of Belmont, Indiana off of Indiana Route 46, is now a state memorial. Many people feel that Glen Cooper Henshaw of Nashville, vies Steele for the honor of Indiana's greatest artist.

Indiana doesn't have to take a back seat when it comes to movie stars. Elmo Lincoln from Rochester played Tarzan on the silent screen. He was followed by such greats as Cliffton Webb of Indianapolis, Marjorie Main of Action, Forest Tucker of Plainfield, Carole (Peters) Lombard of Fort Wayne, Irene Dunn of Madison, James Dean of Marion, and Carl Malden of Gary.

Red Skelton of Vincennes, Phil Harris of Linton, and the late Herb Shriner, who wasn't a native Hoosier, but wouldn't let you forget his Indiana background, are names that rank at the top in the world of comedy.

Richard Bennett, Florence Henderson, Myron McCormick, and Forest